P9-EDZ-528

"As Prime Minister, I Would…"

CANADA'S BRIGHTEST OFFER

INNOVATIVE SOLUTIONS

FOR A MORE PROSPEROUS AND

UNITED COUNTRY

VOLUME TWO

"As Prime Minister, I Would…"

CANADA'S BRIGHTEST OFFER

INNOVATIVE SOLUTIONS

FOR A MORE PROSPEROUS AND

UNITED COUNTRY

MACMILLAN CANADA
TORONTO

Copyright © 1996 Magna International Inc.

All rights reserved. The use of any part of this publication reproduced, trans-mitted in any form or by any means, electronic, mechanical, recording or otherwise, or stored in a retrieval system, without the prior consent of the publisher is an infringement of the copyright law. In the case of photocopying or other reprographic copying of the material, a licence must be obtained from the Canadian Copyright Licensing Agency (CANCOPY) before proceeding.

Canadian Cataloguing in Publication Data

Main entry under title:
As prime Minister I would—

ISBN 0–7715–7409–6 (v. 2)

1. Canada—Politics and government—1993–   .*
2. Canada—Social policy.   3. Canada—Economic policy—1991–   .
I. Stronach, Frank.
FC635.A72   1995   971.064'8   C95–932549–2
F1034.2.A72   1995

Design: Kevin Connolly

Text Composition/Scans: IBEX Graphic Communications Inc.

Macmillan Canada
A Division of Canada Publishing Corporation
Toronto, Ontario, Canada

1 2 3 4 5 B 00 99 98 97 96

Printed and bound in Canada

AUGUSTANA LIBRARY
UNIVERSITY OF ALBERTA

Contents

The world is full of critics, and there are plenty of people who have opinions. But there are very few people who have solutions and the courage to submit those ideas to public scrutiny.

We salute the students and the other writers for their participation in this program and their courage in searching for solutions. They have done so in the spirit of serving their country, so that all Canadians might benefit from their ideas.

Frank Stronach

Magna For Canada Scholarship Fund Acknowledgements

The Magna For Canada Scholarship Fund wishes to acknowledge the contributions of the following people:

The Co-Chairs

Dennis Mills, M.P.
Broadview-Greenwood

Belinda Stronach
Vice-President, Magna International Inc.

The Board of Governors

Michael Burns
Executive Director, Ontario Undergraduate Student Alliance

Michel Gervais
Rector, Université de Laval

Nancy Greene-Raine
Former World and Canadian Olympic Ski Champion
1995 Magna For Canada Scholarship Award Invitational Winner

John Oakley
CFRB Radio Talk Show Host

Dr. Elizabeth Parr-Johnston
President and Vice-Chancellor, Mt. St. Vincent University

J. Robert Prichard
President, University of Toronto

Royden Richardson
Secretary and Director, Richardson Greenshields of Canada Limited

The 1996 National Panel of Judges

Patrick Boyer, Q.C.
President, Breakout Educational Network

Michael Burns
Executive Director, Ontario Undergraduate Student Alliance

Nancy Greene-Raine
Former World and Canadian Olympic Ski Champion

Wade MacLauchlan
Dean of Law, University of New Brunswick

James Nicol
Chairman, TRIAM Automotive Inc.

John Oakley
CFRB Radio Talk Show Host

Jocelyne Pelchat
Chair, Université de Québec a Montréal
President, Pelchat International

The Members of the 1996 Magna For Canada Scholarship Fund Organizing Committee

Eva Gaspar
Keith Stein
Paul Pivato
Colleen Walsh

The 1996 Magna For Canada Scholarship Awards Student Participants

All the students from across Canada who took the time and effort to write proposals that demonstrated a profound concern for the future of our country, and in particular, those recognized below for Honourable Mentions: Todd Guiton, Connie Guss, Charles Lafortune, Andy Lamey, Marc-André Marcotte, Scott Murray, Mathew O'Halloran, Brian Orend, Robert Reilly and Ryan Schnieder.

Magna For Canada
Scholarship Awards Program
Judging Process

The winning student proposals contained in this book were selected by a distinguished national panel of judges representing different regions of the country. The panel was comprised of judges with accomplished backgrounds in business, academia, media and government affairs.

The national panel met with more than forty students whose papers were deemed to be among the best submissions received by the Scholarship Fund. Each student gave an oral synopsis of his or her proposal and was then interviewed by the panel.

The judges selected as the ten Regional Winners students whose proposals contained the most innovative and workable solutions and students who demonstrated a high degree of poise, knowledge and skill during the interview sessions.

One of the ten Regional Winners was declared the National Winner at a Gala Awards Evening, held at Roy Thomson Hall in Toronto on October 25, 1996.

THE 1995 MAGNA FOR CANADA SCHOLARSHIP AWARDS NATIONAL WINNER

Trevor Moat was selected as the 1995 National Winner for his proposal, "A Vision of National Unity and Improved Living Standards in Canada." The Carleton University student, currently completing a Master's degree in systems and computer engineering, advocated a national system of rotating annual elections at each level of government in order to ensure continuous voter feedback and greater political accountability.

The 1996 National Champion will be identified in a publication to be produced next year.

DISCLAIMER

The ideas contained in this book have been published to stimulate debate and are not necessarily the views of Magna International Inc., its Chairman, Frank Stronach, or the Fair Enterprise Institute.

Foreword

The world is changing rapidly, and there's a great trend today toward global economies. What does this mean? More specifically, is it good for Canadians? Is it bad for Canadians? The plain fact is that globalization gives business more freedom to move about. Business has one mandate: to make a profit. And money has no heart, no soul, no conscience, and no homeland. It flows through the path of least resistance.

The natural outcome of this trend is greater global competition for goods and services, which in itself is a good thing and could serve to improve the living standards of people everywhere throughout the world. But greater competition also means that countries that are overtaxed and overgoverned—countries such as Canada—are being adversely affected by the trend toward globalization, as business increasingly moves to lower-tax, lower-cost countries that offer potentially greater returns. This trend will further accelerate the decline in Canadian living standards.

It is extremely important, therefore, that we as Canadians take a hard look at ourselves, recognize our problems, and develop action plans to correct those shortcomings. Problems never go away of their own accord. On the contrary, if left unchecked, they grow in size and severity. We need to analyze our total system, especially in regards to how the country is governed. It becomes quickly apparent, upon taking a close look, that many aspects of our system are badly flawed.

Take, for example, our parliamentary system. Government should be the management team of a country. Unfortunately, that management team is made up of politicians, and the primary mandate of a politician is to be elected or re-elected. That means that our country is managed to a great extent by political rather than economic priorities.

It would seem obvious, therefore, that we devise a new system that would balance the present political management and allow for a more economically driven agenda. We need to replace the politically appointed Senate with a chamber of non-partisan citizen representatives elected in a non-political process. These citizens would have a full vote on key legislative bills and would act as an effective check on the power of the governing party. Citizen representatives would be much more inclined to place the country's economic welfare and long-term national interests ahead of political considerations or partisan views.

Canadians expect the federal government to lay down rules and regulations and uphold standards in regards to health, education, and the environment. But they also expect government to live within its means. The fact is that governments cannot spend more than they take in. And our governments have been doing that for quite some time now. Government spending in Canada has gone way out of line and our debt continues to climb, yet our governments continue to act as though they were somehow immune from the same economic laws that govern our lives.

Consider the simple analogy of a household budget. When a family spends more than it makes, it must reduce spending. If the family does not cut back, the household inevitably goes broke. The same basic principle holds true for businesses and governments. If a government continually spends more money than it is able to collect by taxation or other means, the country will eventually face bankruptcy. In the case of a country, the government can prolong the process by printing more money. But in the final analysis, if a country spends more than it generates in revenue, the country will inevitably go broke.

The recent efforts at trimming our large budget deficit are hardly cause for celebration. The Canadian ship of state continues to take on water, and if the debt continues to rise there exists the very real possibility that the ship will go under. We must take bolder action to prevent Canada from sinking into insolvency. We need to begin by reducing government overhead and by dismantling our massive bureaucracy. In short, we need to rethink and restructure the way in which government works. Reducing the size of government does not mean that we would become lax with regard to upholding federal standards in areas such as health and the environment. Nor should the burden of government restructuring be carried solely by our civil servants; we must guard against making bureaucrats the scapegoats for our financial problems. However, by eliminating waste and gradually phasing out unnecessary services, we could dramatically lower government overhead. More important, we would eliminate the red tape and bureaucratic roadblocks that add to the cost of doing business and impede growth. Once the annual deficit was eliminated, we would begin generating a yearly surplus that could be utilized to pay down the national debt. For the first time in nearly a generation, our government would operate a balanced budget and Canadians would enjoy the prospect of improved living standards.

Another area that clearly needs reform is our tax and financial system. A significant amount of capital is sucked out of the financial markets by governments issuing bonds and other debt instruments. Governments should be prohibited from issuing bonds unless the funds are specifically raised for national infrastructure projects, with clear guidelines preventing state or private monopoly control. As it now stands, those who purchase government bonds receive, in many cases, a greater return than those who run the risk of investing in private enterprise. Why would a business person in Canada invest money in setting up shop, buying equipment and machinery, hiring employees, and coping with a suffocating bureaucracy, when that person can just as easily buy government bonds? We have created a system that no longer rewards those business people and entrepreneurs who take a financial risk and create the wealth and the jobs this country so badly needs.

Our tax system must be geared toward the creation and fair distribution of wealth. In a free society, the best way to create wealth is through increased productivity, and the best way for a nation to be more productive is for employees to receive a fair share of the wealth they help to create. A tax system that encouraged this sort of profit sharing would help stimulate the biggest economic boom this country has ever experienced.

Given the many problems that confront us, where do we go from here? History has proven that the establishment is content with the status quo. But for many Canadians—especially young Canadians—the status quo no longer works. Most Canadian students realize that it has become increasingly difficult to get a job, and they also know that creating more government jobs would only dig this country deeper in the hole. Many of them realize that by clinging to the status quo, their future is bleak.

It is for these young Canadians that we have created the Magna For Canada Scholarship Fund, an annual awards program designed to provide a national forum for Canadian college and university students to express their hopes, dreams, and ideas for a more prosperous and united country.

The best proposals put forth by students from across the country are contained in this year's collection of winning essays, together with the proposals of a number of distinguished Canadians from various parts of the country and various backgrounds. It is our hope that these proposals will spark among Canadians a constructive debate focused on renewing our federation, especially among students, who traditionally have been in the vanguard of social reform and political change.

The Magna For Canada Scholarship Fund is attempting to build a platform for a new kind of social revolution—a revolution of the mind, a peaceful and progressive revolution working with the tools of democracy.

Despite the problems that beset us, Canada still has much to be proud of: there are many things we do exceedingly well. People everywhere admire and praise our clean and safe communities, our virtues of decency, law, and order, and our tolerance for diversity of peoples and opinions. We have a tradition of respect for individual freedoms and rights, and a concern for the environment.

It would be a tragedy to watch our country slide into further economic decline without struggling to identify and correct the problems that have bottlenecked progress for the past several decades. I urge all Canadians to work at reinforcing the economic fabric of our country, because that fabric is unravelling at a much quicker pace than many people realize. By tackling some of the problems I have outlined, the country could become more efficient and productive, and the national debt could be eliminated in a relatively short period of time. We could develop a solid economic framework that would allow us to take care of all those who cannot take care of themselves.

But to do so we must move away from the priorities of partisan politics and toward the realities of global economics. I am confident we can rise to the challenge, and in so doing, regain our stature as a leading economic nation.

Frank Stronach
Toronto
August 26, 1996

PART ONE

Winning Student Ideas

Hands Off! The Case for Privatization and the "Undoing" of Government

JASON BROOKS

JASON BROOKS

A resident of Burlington, Ontario, Jason is in the second year of the journalism program at Carleton University in Ottawa. While at Carleton, he has served on the executive of the University Progressive Conservative Association and written numerous articles for several school newspapers as well as *The Ottawa Citizen*. While in high school, Jason founded the Progressive Conservative Youth Association in his home riding. A budding entrepreneur, he also started two businesses: a dry-cleaning company, which he later sold, and a window-cleaning business, which he still operates during the summer.

With any change in government, there comes, with rather obvious inevitability, the promise of change. On meeting this promise, I hope it would be said of me as Prime Minister that "with breathtaking fervour did he complete his task." This zealous desire to change the country has its roots in my belief that there are many things wrong with the country as it currently exists. Our standard of living is threatened by ever-increasing taxes, government debt, and a failing healthcare system. The very future of the country hangs in balance, as anxiety about separation has "highjacked" our national political agenda. It is my view that the problems we face—threats to our standard of living and to national unity—can be traced to one common, fundamental cause: that our liberal system of government, established in the Lockean tradition of the protection of life, liberty, and property, has extended its powers of "protection" so far that it threatens to smother all that is worth protecting. As the antithesis to the current situation, I put forward my own system of beliefs, which, while natural and obvious to me, has been lost on previous governments. In short, I believe that people ought to be free to run their lives as they choose. In Canada today, the size and scope of our federal government have taken away these natural rights to choose and, consequently, stand as the problem rather than the solution to challenges of improving living standards and unifying Canadians. We have reached the point at which it could be said of governments that the true measure of their success lies, or ought to lie, not in what they do, but rather in what they undo.

Improving Living Standards

The first step in "undoing" Canada as we know it would be a massive privatization of nearly all federal government operations. I have often joked privately that if I were elected Prime Minister, I would sit down with each member of my Cabinet and explain that the prime objective of each member is to leave no job for the minister who will succeed him or her. While this may be an oversimplification, it is not far from where I actually stand. If we really want to increase the standard of living in this country, it is imperative that we reduce the size of government through privatization. First, privately run institutions, because they are driven by the profit motive, are able to perform the same functions as public institutions at a much higher degree of efficiency. The nature of competitive markets ensures that operations that are not conducted with maximum efficiency will be replaced by those that are. Privatization of government would result in immediate cost savings purely from increases in operational efficiency. Second, products that the public does not consider worth what it currently pays for them indirectly through taxes will cease to be delivered. Faced with the real costs of what they buy, people will suddenly be able to weigh real costs against real benefits and make rational purchasing decisions based on their wants, needs, and ability to pay. This is not done at present, as the government effectively forces everyone to buy things that the government, rather than the people, feels should be purchased. Privatization, then, of virtually all government operations—from foreign aid to the CBC—would in effect put out of business all operations that the market does not want, and make more efficient the ones that it does. Under such a system of reduced government, people will be free to purchase any of the products that the government currently supplies—from donating money to developing nations to financing the CBC. The difference is that people won't have to. In short, they will spend their money where they want to. As a result, privatization will increase living standards for Canadian society, as we will get more of what we want and less of what we do not.

Government should next shed itself of its responsibilities in the area of transferring money to individuals. Unemployment insurance and the Canada Pension Plan would, like much else, work better under private-sector direction. The privatization of unemployment insurance would make it more like home insurance and less like welfare. People would be forced to pay its real costs and not expect subsidized perks. This would discourage abuse of the system and reduce the inefficiency caused by a system that too often encourages the very unemployment whose effects it aims to cushion. Private insurers, driven by a profit motive, would naturally provide a greater incentive to encourage their customers to keep themselves employed; similarly, faced with the real costs of insurance, many people may choose not to buy insurance at all, giving themselves the ultimate incentive to stay employed. Either way, there would be more encouragement for people to maintain employment, and this would have the effect of raising national income and thus living standards, as defined in economic terms.

The current unfunded liability on the Canada Pension Plan, which is in the hundreds of billions of dollars, suggests that the government is no better at running a pension plan than it is at running anything else. The Canada Pension Plan should be taken out of the hands of the government and people should be left to pay into their own private pension plans—thus ensuring that the money will not be misplaced or misspent by government. The only role for the government in the private pension plan system would be to pass legislation that forces people to pay into their private plans. Without this provision, we might expect that large numbers of people would neglect to provide for their retirement, and governments, faced in time with an impoverished group of elderly, would provide them with assistance out of compassion (and a desire for votes)—with the losers being those who prudently paid into their own pensions and now must pay for the pensions of others. In all fairness, forcing people to pay into their own private pensions is a justifiable infringement by government.

After transfers to persons are sufficiently dealt with, government should get out of the business of subsidizing provinces. Equalization payments that provide subsidization to poorer provinces do more harm than good. The inherent problem with subsidization of any kind is that it encourages both an overuse and underuse of resources at the same time. By providing extra market funding to provinces where productivity is poor, the problem of poverty is only perpetuated by encouraging people to live and work where it would not otherwise be as economically viable. The removal of subsidization would cause people in subsidized areas to face the real costs of their situation; many might then choose to relocate to industries or regions where their labour would be in greater demand. In subsidizing inefficient areas of the country, the federal government also causes underuse of resources in areas of more efficiency, for by virtue of subsidization, money is diverted from more economically profitable expenditures. In the subsidization game, inefficiency means that we are all losers in the long run.

Beyond cuts to equalization, all transfers to provinces should be reduced, if not eliminated entirely. Provinces would then raise their spending money directly through their own taxes. A more competitive tax market would evolve, with businesses and individuals drawn to provinces where rates are most favourable. Presumably lower taxes would result, allowing Canadians to keep more of their money and spend it according to their individual priorities—again, increasing the efficiency in resource allocation and, with it, living standards.

While close to the hearts of most Canadians, our state of public health care needs to be reworked. Increasing demand for services and decreasing ability of the government to supply these services have left us with one of the typical inefficiencies of any state-run enterprise: line-ups. The *Canada Health Act* must be amended to allow the sale of private medical services in this country. The public system must continue to exist—it is not only inhumane by Canadian standards to deny people essential health care on the basis of their wealth, but no government that realistically expects to get re-elected can have people dying in the streets. A two-tiered system, however, allowing those with money to purchase private health care, would work towards keeping our best doctors and the lucrative healthcare industry from migrating south of the border, while also relieving pressure on the line-ups for the public system. Since those purchasing private health care would necessarily continue to pay into the public system through their taxes, the result of a two-tiered system would be increased freedom and health care not only for the wealthy but also for the non-wealthy, as the amount of money in the public system would be retained at current levels but will service a smaller number of people. A two-tiered system would be acceptable, even to Canadians, as quality levels would be increased in both systems—public and private—leading to better health care for all.

With a massive downsizing of government, a large portion of our tax burden would be replaced by fees charged by the private sector—we would pay for things on a per-use basis as with much of what we buy. It would be nice to eliminate all taxes for, by their nature, they discourage productivity and encourage a misallocation of resources. Unfortunately, this is unrealistic. There are huge payments remaining to be made on our national debt and, furthermore, there will continue to be several areas of government, such as the Department of National Defence, for which privatization is likely neither feasible nor desirable in the foreseeable future. Taxes of some sort will persist. We can, however, mitigate the inefficiency and unfairness, which siphon away potential productivity, that can be found within our current tax system. To this end, I would immediately opt for a flat consumption-based tax (an expanded goods and services tax) in place of our current progressive income tax system. This would eliminate the disincentives caused by moving through different income tax brackets, and relieve thousands of brilliant minds from their unproductive toil in the zero-sum industries of tax avoidance and tax collection. Many tax collectors, tax accountants, and tax lawyers would be displaced from this wasteland of redundant transfer of wealth into industries of actual wealth creation. A simpler, smaller, more efficient tax system would raise national productivity and lead to a betterment of the economic condition of most Canadians.

National Unity

While many of the objectives I have outlined go far in encouraging increased living standards, they do not ostensibly address the unity problem that looms large on the national political scene. But, in fact, they do—for while we weren't looking, the unity situation actually solved itself. Allow me to offer a systematic analysis, beginning with what I believe the government should not do.

Government cannot and should not in my opinion, preserve political bonds, by means of force or other coercion, with a people who wish to sever these bonds. This is consistent with my view that people ought to be able to make for themselves the decisions that shape their lives. Certainly, the people of Quebec ought to be entirely free to separate if they so choose. In today's world of open borders, the separation of Quebec would not even be a necessarily bad thing—in fact, it would be relatively neutral: a best-case scenario would see free trade prevail, with separation achieving little of substance aside from some intangible wound that would be inflicted upon an equally intangible national pride, and, of course, the end of lucrative equalization payments to Quebec. So the prospect of Quebec's separation, in principle, does not bother me, for the simple reason that I am not a nationalist but an individualist.

Of course, there are a few sticky points that would accompany any separation. First, there would emerge a seemingly endless sea of constitutional wrangling between Quebec and the rest of Canada over the logistics of separation that would, by comparison, make Meech Lake look like a puddle. This would be followed by the equally redundant zero-sum game of re-establishing economic and other ties at a level desired by the two separate polities. Second, there arises the hypothetical challenge that many federalists see as their trump card: if Canada is divisible, then so too is Quebec. If we were to follow this logic, what would emerge would be an endless number of tiny self-governing nations (regions, cities—indeed, any property-owning citizen would be able to declare himself or herself sovereign), all linked together in a common-market economic union. The formation of these tiny nations would provide, if nothing else, a lot of work for a lot of lawyers.

So, if with the relative destruction of the powers of the federal government and the formation of a relatively loose, decentralized economic union are the end result of a separation process, there are two roads by which to arrive at this end. The first is the rather untidy process of separation, which would entail at least another referendum, potentially confrontational negotiations, and many uncertainties. This process would lead, at least in the short term, to a perception of political and market instability by international investors, and hence a rise in interest rates, a decline in investment, and, in general, economic loss.

The second route to resolution would be a simple devolution of powers—the federal government unilaterally strips itself to a bare-bones position, giving over much of its enormous power to the private sector, and thus to individual citizens. This second route would skirt around the uncertainties of political separation, would save the logistical hassles of separation and a subsequent renegotiation of economic ties and, most of all, would actually elate rather than alarm international investors by constituting a shift toward free-market economics. In short, the policies of government reduction outlined earlier would, without even explicitly trying, deflate any and all arguments presented by Quebec's separatist movement and, in fact, rescue us from the unity "crisis" in which, by some accounts, we currently find ourselves drowning.

Certainly, there are a number of things wrong with Canada as it presently exists, and change, while desirable, must come with an intensity not often seen in modern times. Because the problems that face our nation stem from a fundamental view of what the role of government should be, basic ways of thinking must be changed. No longer do we benefit from an increased role by the government in our lives—in fact, a huge privatization of government functions and a more hands-off approach to issues such as health care and taxation actually carry the promise of great gains to Canadian society—both in terms of living standards and of national unity. To deliver this promise requires politicians—indeed, citizens—who dare to be courageous, free-thinking, and willing to change a nation by "undoing" its government. It is my sincere hope that enough such people exist.

Winds of Change: A Proposal for Political and Economic Renewal in Canada

MICHAEL FRIEDMAN

MICHAEL FRIEDMAN

Michael is entering his fourth year of study at the University of Toronto, where he is pursuing a minor in political science and a minor in economics. A resident of Toronto, he was the host of a community sports television program and worked for two years as a volunteer in the emergency room of a local hospital. He also took part in the University of Toronto mentorship program and wrote for *The Varsity*, University of Toronto's student newspaper. Last year he served as an intern in the office of Mayor Mel Lastman in the City of North York. A University of Toronto scholar, Michael is the winner of numerous university scholarships and awards.

In virtually unprecedented fashion, the Canadian polis has been confronted by a series of dehabilitating social and economic trends that threaten to challenge the very sanctity of the Canadian state. Crippled by decades of gross economic mismanagement and a reprehensible disregard for the country's fragile national mosaic, successive governments of all partisan stripes have thrust the nation to the verge of political collapse. Perpetual resistance provided by Quebec nationalists, coupled with the collective evils of debt financing and increased level of influence exercised by international financiers, has exacerbated the tensions that have undermined all recent attempts to govern in a compassionate, yet fiscally conservative, manner. While it would be irresponsible to contend that Canada's volatile political landscape can be readily tamed by a series of cursory, short-term solutions, a concerted attempt at substantive reform could enjoy a significant degree of success if capable of tapping into the rustic ingenuity that single-handedly stimulated the early development of the nation-at-large. Consequently, if I were granted the opportunity to serve as Prime Minister of Canada, I would enact the following reforms, aimed jointly at improving the living standards of all citizens and at promoting a far more inclusive, unified national ethos.

National Unity

Central to the continued survival of the Canadian state is the need to reinvigorate the ties that bind together the country's five unique regions. Undermined by a legislative system that piously focuses on the will of the absolute majority, governments—both past and present—have blatantly disregarded the need to grant regional concerns an effective voice in the ongoing discussion of public policy. In an effort to represent the collective views of the Canadian electorate better, the following constitutional amendments would directly facilitate a shift toward a more unified national spirit.

Tripartite Confederate Assembly

Originally designed to reflect the views of the propertied class and provide a chamber of solemn analysis, the country's appointed Senate no longer stands as an influential fixture on the Canadian political scene. Overshadowed by the domineering strength of the elected House of Commons, the Senate has, in practical terms, lost the ability to question fundamentally the efficacy of federal legislative acts.

Over the past several years, the concept of a "Triple-E" Senate has been proposed by groups of varying political orientations as a possible improvement to the country's archaic administrative structure. Predicated upon the assumption that regional interests have fallen victim to the overbearing strength of the representational blocs from Ontario and Quebec, the Triple-E model is designed to grant Canada's less-populated regions the power to contribute meaningfully to the development of federal legislation. By declaring that the Senate enjoy substantive power in drafting and approving federal acts of Parliament while drawing its representatives equally from throughout the nation, the Triple-E Senate has been lauded as the cornerstone of a fundamentally superior form of representational democracy.

Nevertheless, given Canada's highly centralized population base and the consequent resistance to any attempt to attenuate the current balance of governing power, it is highly unlikely that the Triple-E concept would be capable of garnering the support necessary to guide such an ambitious plan to fruition. By contrast, a mode of Senate reform that respects the need to recognize the pre-eminence of the absolute majority will more accurately address the divisive nature of the contemporary legislative system and, by extension, appeal to a larger cross-section of Canadian society.

The Tripartite Confederate Assembly would overcome the shortcomings of all previous models by drawing representatives from not only the electorate at large, but also from all provincial administrations. The Assembly would consist of 90 sitting members, 55 of whom would be equally divided among Canada's five distinct socio-geographic regions, 12 of whom would act as appointed representatives of each provincial and territorial government, five of whom would exclusively represent the interests of the country's Aboriginal peoples, and a final 18 representatives, each elected on a strictly proportional basis.[1] The new Upper House would boast the distinct advantage of reflecting the interests of all Canadians, including the often neglected views of the country's large body of Aboriginal peoples, while continuing to place an appropriate emphasis on the sentiments of those residing in the nation's most populated regions.

The constitutional amendments that would culminate in the formation of the Tripartite Confederate Assembly would also need to address the unbalanced relationship between the House of Commons and the Senate. Notwithstanding senators' formal ability to challenge legislation passed in the House of Commons, the fact that they are appointed and do not represent the will of a particular constituency undermines any claim that the Senate acts as an effective guardian of the Canadian populace. By contrast, the Assembly would be empowered to contest the validity of all federal legislation forcefully and table bills that suit the interests of members' own constituencies.[2] Given that almost 75 percent of the seats in the Assembly are divided equally among the country's five regions, it would act as a powerful wedge against the centrally dominated House of Commons.

In fairness to the precept of majority rule—the bedrock upon which the concept of popular democracy rests—the House of Commons would be empowered to override an Assembly veto (possibly with a two-thirds majority in a general House vote). Nonetheless, the Tripartite Confederate Assembly would stand as an influential force on the federal political scene, providing a visible platform for the healthy discussion of regional issues.

Constitutional Division of Powers

The legislative division of powers, as outlined in sections 91 and 92 of the *Constitution Act, 1867,* no longer accurately reflects the true scope of services that need to be provided on a national level and those that are best provided on a regional level. In the hope of maintaining a cohesive and functional federation, both the provincial and federal levels of government must endeavour to operate in a manner that allows for services to be provided in the most efficient manner possible, while simultaneously respecting the customs, priorities, and traditions of the people of each individual province. As a result, sections 91 and 92 of the *Constitution Act* must be amended in order to clarify the legislative jurisdiction of each level of government.

While the federal government will still retain unfettered authority over interprovincial trade, national defence, immigration policy, and all other matters that are truly "national" in character, the enumeration of areas under provincial jurisdiction as outlined in section 92 will be rightly expanded. Under the new division of powers, each of Canada's provinces would gain greater control over such controversial areas as labour law, regional development, and telecommunications. On account of the new reforms, the constitutional division of powers will settle at a more even balance, building the foundation for closer ties between the federal and provincial governments in the years to come.

With the establishment of the Tripartite Confederate Assembly and an appropriate realignment of the federal–provincial division of powers, the views and beliefs of all Canadians, regardless of their geographic location, will receive the attention and respect they so duly deserve. In turn, on account of the reforms suggested above, the ongoing quest to secure a stable national union will be notably furthered.

Canadian Living Standards

Despite the arguments of those firmly committed to the contractionist economic philosophy of the 1990s, it is possible to increase the country's overall standard of living without neglecting the government's obligation to bring its financial house to order. However, unlike the costly, state-dominated social welfare programs of the 1950s, Canada's new economic realities dictate that any attempt to better the collective lot of the general populace must focus primarily upon the reallocation of existing resources, rather than the introduction of further state programming.

National Youth Corps

Central to any attempt to improve Canadian living standards is the government's ability to integrate the nation's youth into the management and preservation of their own communities better. Crime, illiteracy, and gross poverty stand as monumental barriers, bound to encumber any bid to improve the lives of all Canadians successfully. The only conceivable way to shatter the destructive cycle that has ravaged select groups of young Canadians is to provide those subjugated pockets of society with the opportunity to build a foundation for social betterment out of the ashes of personal defeat and despair. By creating a program committed to allowing youth to work in their communities and to improve the appearance and quality of life in their neighbourhoods, the government will take the first step toward reinvigorating our local townships from coast to coast.

The National Youth Corps will group teenagers in grades eight through 10 with responsible community leaders and university students who will be charged with leading their "teams" in both recreational and "local action" activities. The Corps will serve the joint purpose of allowing teens to socialize with their peers in a constructive environment while making a contribution to the maintenance and growth of their communities. Local-action activities, ranging from gardening and delivery services for senior citizens to environmental clean-up programs at regional parks and conservation areas, will allow the nation's youth to gain a greater respect for their neighbourhoods and experience the joy associated with improving the lives of their fellow people.

When fully implemented, the National Youth Corps will constitute the first step in the country's revised battle plan against the social ills that have crippled the productive vitality of Canada's younger generations. By showing all young Canadians that they can make a productive contribution to the growth of our nation, irrespective of their innate intellectual or physical abilities, the Corps will inspire teenagers across the country to continue to strive for personal excellence. With proper encouragement, the synergy of collective action will propel youngsters beyond the evils of crime and self-destructive action and create a pool of eager and aggressive workers, ready to lead Canada triumphantly into the 21st century.

Education Reform—A "Public–Private" Partnership

Inextricably linked to the ideals that underlie the National Youth Corps stands the concept of self-betterment. The role of Canada's public school boards is to provide students with the tools necessary to adapt successfully to the ever-changing job market. Unfortunately, far too often, the needs of the student and the evolving characteristics of the private marketplace are ignored in a flawed effort to maintain a common curriculum. Similarly, a lack of communication between school board administrators and local business people has created an incongruence between the skills taught at school and those demanded in the workplace. As a consequence, in order to improve the living standards of younger Canadians, the operation of our school systems must be drastically altered.

An active bond needs to be forged between the nation's school boards and the industries that comprise the private sector. With the onslaught of automated computer technology, the curriculum of the country's elementary and secondary schools must be aligned with the changing needs of Canadian business. In order to ensure that the country's youth have a reasonable chance of achieving prosperity in their adulthood, the process of curriculum development must be transformed into a full-fledged public–private partnership. Furthermore, the expansion of joint educational ventures including, most notably, the extremely successful cooperative education program, will help to acclimatize students to the highly competitive world of work, while allowing them to master the skills necessary to succeed in the hostile employment market of the 1990s.

The Environmental Action Bill

Notwithstanding the benefits that accrue from financial gain, the natural environment plays a dominant role in determining the quality of life that Canadians have grown to enjoy. With the increased production of pollutants and toxins threatening our natural ecosystems, significant steps must be taken to protect the country's fragile habitat.

The Environmental Action Bill consists of a two-pronged approach to tackling the devastating effects of environmental degradation. On the one hand, the Bill offers financial inducements, including tax credits and government grants, to any business that endeavours to make use of new equipment deemed to be of a more "environmentally friendly" nature. It will also empower the government to provide further subsidies to any domestic manufacturer specializing in the production of equipment aimed at pollution reduction.

In a similar vein, the Bill will utilize the force of the law to penalize those who, willingly or unwillingly, damage the natural environment. Unlike the hollow legislative initiatives of the past, the Environmental Action Bill will prescribe mandatory prison sentences, coupled with significant financial penalties, for those companies that fail to satisfy yearly environmental guidelines as set out by the federal government. To administer the new program, an arm's-length federal department will be created and will report directly to the House of Commons twice each year.

Upon the full enactment of the Bill, businesses will finally be rewarded for operating in an environmentally responsible manner. Conversely, those corporations that refuse to respect the sanctity of our air and water supplies will be penalized to the full extent of the law.

Economic Expansion Initiative

An extremely troubling wave of industrial and corporate downsizing has recently cast a dark shadow over Canada's once impressive pattern of sustained economic development. In an effort to combat the ravages of a prolonged recession and survive in the increasingly competitive international marketplace, firms have been forced to resort to drastic austerity measures in order to maintain acceptable profit margins. Unfortunately, while such downsizing measures have helped to satisfy corporations' short-term economic objectives, the Canadian corporate sector is now incapable of devoting the resources necessary to secure the long-term economic opportunities that are crucial to ensuring the continued growth of the Canadian private sector. Accordingly, the federal government must drastically alter the Canadian tax code in order to stimulate the consistent and robust expansion of the national economy.

In the hope of leading Canadian business along a path of sustained growth, the Economic Expansion Initiative will eliminate all corporate taxes on revenues that exceed a firm's earnings for the previous year multiplied by a variable growth factor.[3] Specifically, the government will endeavour not to tax increases in corporate revenues, thereby fuelling the drive toward corporate expansion. Moreover, given the use of the variable-growth factor, the federal government will still retain the control necessary to tailor the level of tax relief provided to the current state of the Canadian economy (for example, in periods of high economic growth, the percentage of increase in gross domestic product included in the variable-growth factor could be increased).

The adoption of the Economic Expansion Initiative will re-establish the importance of sustained corporate growth to the continued prosperity of the nation in aggregate. By focusing the government's fiscal efforts squarely on a mechanism that champions economic expansion, the contemporary emphasis on downsizing will be replaced by a spirit of increased opportunity culminating in the continued enhancement of Canadian living standards.

Conclusion

Without question, the task of improving both the living standards of all Canadians and the unity of the country as a whole is far more complex than one can convey in a short, written proposal. However, the initiatives outlined above do address the most significant challenges facing Canadians as we collectively prepare to enter the new millennium. Canada's long-standing sectional cleavages, coupled with the new economic realities associated with increased global competition, necessitate some form of substantive government action. In turn, the series of reforms detailed in the preceding sections stand as a perfect antidote to the ailments afflicting our once vibrant nation.

Notes

1. Eighteen members would be divided among the four most populated provinces (according to the most recent census data).

2. With the exception of "supply bills."
3. The variable-growth factor will likely represent one plus a certain percentage of the growth in the nation's gross domestic product (for example, if GDP expands by 3 percent and two thirds of GDP expansion is scheduled to be incorporated into the mechanism of the Economic Expansion Initiative, the variable-growth factor for that particular year would be 1.02).

Laying to Rest Partisan Politics: The Prerequisite for a Mature Society

JEFF WOOD

JEFF WOOD

A resident of Brockville, Ontario, Jeff is beginning the first year of a Master of Science in Civil Engineering at the University of Waterloo. He holds a Bachelor of Science in Civil Engineering from the University of Waterloo. He is a past participant in the Canada World Youth Program, and took part in an eight-month exchange program with the University of Tottori in Japan. Jeff is a member of the Kitchener-Waterloo Philharmonic Choir and the Wilfred Laurier University Choir. He enjoys reading and gardening.

Partisan politics have been a fact of life in Canada since the country was founded almost 130 years ago. Working within the parliamentary system borrowed from the British, political parties of the past have helped to define our country by giving us a means to organize ourselves and express our various points of view.

In recent years, however, Canadians have become increasingly cynical about our political system. The media have played a significant, if unwitting, part in this trend. Through newsprint, radio, television, and now the Internet, Canadians now have the ability to peer into the innermost workings of government and observe our elected representatives at their enlightened best and their ignorant and vindictive worst.

For most of us, this ability to observe the political process closely has not come without a cost. Many of us are discouraged by what we see happening in our governing bodies, and the media seem quite happy to present us with the worst news about our leaders that they can find. As a result, we have become increasingly confused, angry, and disillusioned with our political leaders. At best, we have lost our innocence and naiveté, and, at worst, become jaded and fatalistic about our future as a nation.

Many people have recognized this trend and have attempted to capitalize on it. Political spin-doctors have been among the best at sniffing the political winds and steering their parties in new, and sometimes unpalatable, directions. Major transformations on the political scene have occurred, with one national political party teetering on the brink of irrelevancy and two other parties with narrower, regional focuses springing forth to capitalize on the anger and divisiveness that are currently sweeping across the country. It could even be argued that in some cases these new political parties pander to our fear of change and mistrust of diversity in an effort to gain more and more power.

Instead of allowing our country to continue its spiral into pettiness and mediocrity, I believe that we must act decisively to restore our political process to high regard and give it the support and input it needs to deal with the challenges that we face, both now and in the future. The only way to accomplish such a transformation is, in my view, to restore the control of the government to the people of Canada by taking it away from those who currently hold it: the political parties of Canada.

The Problems with Partisan Politics

Despite the credit due to partisan forces in shaping what is now modern Canada, the disadvantages are now beginning to outweigh the advantages. My biggest concern about partisan politics is its adversarial nature. Today's politicians, it seems, are more concerned with discrediting their political opponents and guarding against political attacks than dealing with the problems that face our society. The depths to which they have fallen, with their public bickering, name-calling, and pettiness, would be amusing, if it weren't for the fact that these are the people who are supposed to be watching out for our best interests. At a time when we are encouraged to solve our problems using win–win solutions, our politicians are working within a framework that seems diametrically opposed to such an ideology, and we— at least some of us[1]—will continue to lose.

Another concern is that partisan politics tend, in my view, to take too much of the responsibility of running the government away from society. I think of political parties as corporations that vie with each other to do the job of running the country and, once they win (get elected), do their best to keep Canadians in the dark about what is going on. Like any corporation, each political party demands compensation (usually in the form of power, prestige, and money) and encourages its shareholders (Canadians) to turn a blind eye as it deals with their business (running the country).

Besides being inefficient and politically and socially damaging, this vying between the corporations perpetuates a "back-room" mentality that has, in my view, no place at any level of Canadian government. Voters are not children who must be manipulated for their own (and the party's) good; in fact, a more educated and responsible electorate would be better able to influence the directions our government takes by making thoughtful and informed contributions to the political debate.[2]

In light of these and other concerns, if I were elected Prime Minister I would work to replace our current partisan political process with an efficient, effective, and equitable non-partisan system of government, which, no matter what anyone says, could not realistically be achieved in our current acrimonious and adversarial political landscape.

A New Non-partisan Federal Government

To illustrate how my proposed system might work, let's take the federal governing body as an example. I propose that our new federal government would be made up of a single elected body[3], identified, for the purposes of discussion, as the Federal House of Representatives (see Figure 1).

Members of the Federal House of Representatives

The Federal House of Representatives would be led by a Prime Minister, who would be assisted by two or three Deputy Prime Ministers. Each federal portfolio would be overseen by one Cabinet Minster and three or four Deputy Cabinet Ministers. The rest of the body of the Federal House would be made up by five Public Representatives from each Electoral District.

....

Figure 1: PROPOSED MEMBERSHIP OF THE FEDERAL HOUSE OF REPRESENTATIVES

....

THE CANADIAN FEDERAL HOUSE OF REPRESENTATIVES

Prime Minister

- Full-time position, working in Ottawa
- Serves for four years, then retires
- Elected by the Federal House of Representatives
- Must have served as a Deputy Prime Minister or, if that is not possible (for example, due to illness, resignation), as a Cabinet Minister

Deputy Prime Minister

- Full-time position, working in Ottawa
- Two or three Deputy Prime Ministers, at discretion of Prime Minister
- Serves for four years, then retires (unless promoted)
- Appointed by the Prime Minister as openings become available
- Must have served as a Cabinet Minister

Cabinet Minister

- Full-time position, working in Ottawa
- One Cabinet Minister for each federal portfolio

....

Figure 1 *(continued)*

- Serves for four years, then retires (unless promoted)
- Appointed by the Prime Minister as openings become available
- Must have served as a Deputy Cabinet Minister in any federal portfolio

Deputy Cabinet Minister

- Part-time position, working from home Electoral District
- Three or four Deputy Cabinet Ministers for each portfolio, at the discretion of the Cabinet Minister
- Serves for three years, then retires (unless promoted)
- Appointed by the Cabinet Minister as openings become available
- Must have served as a Public Representative

Public Representative

- Part-time position, working from home Electoral District
- Five Public Representatives for each Electoral District, one elected each year, so that there is a 20-percent turn-over each year
- Serves for five years, then retires (unless promoted)
- Elected by voters in each Electoral District

Beginning Political Service

Each federal politician would begin his or her political service by being elected as a Public Representative for one of the Electoral Districts. The process for conducting such an election would be as follows:

1. Possible candidates for election would be chosen at random from the populace of the Electoral District. Once selected, they would be asked if they would like to be considered as candidates in the upcoming election.

2. Random selection of possible candidates would continue until a given number (20, say) had agreed to run as candidates.

3. Each candidate would present a résumé and a brief explanation of why he or she would like to serve as a Public Representative. This information would be verified by the election committee and made available to the voters through the various media outlets (such as newspapers, World Wide Web pages, and so on).

4. Once the candidate information had been presented to the voters, a series of ballots would then take place to elect the Public Representative. Voting would be done by telephone, television, or computer, with each ballot taking one day. Groups of candidates with the least number of votes would be removed with each successive ballot, and voting would continue until one of the candidates receives a majority of the votes. This candidate would become the next Public Representative for the Electoral District.

Public Representatives

Once elected, the Public Representative would serve for five years, after which he or she would resign and never be eligible for public service again, at any level, unless chosen for higher office (for example, to become a Deputy Cabinet Minister). All Public Representatives would remain in their home Electoral District, where they would work roughly 10 hours each week for a modest honorarium. To allow them to interact with other members of government, a central office would be maintained in each Electoral District with full Internet access, complete with e-mail, multi-party video hook-ups, and World Wide Web access. Some of the advantages to the above system of electing our representatives in government are the following:

- By limiting the service of each Public Representative to five years, we would raise the general level of public awareness about how government works by including more people in it and would prevent politicians from depending on the political process for their livelihood.
- Public Representatives would remain in their own communities, so they would be able to stay closer to their constituents, keep active in their chosen career, and minimize disruption to their families.
- Increasing the numbers of Public Representatives in each Electoral District would give a more balanced representation of Canadian society in the Federal House of Representatives, and allow the new Representatives to learn from their colleagues who have had more experience.
- Reducing the workload of the Public Representatives would help attract people from more varied backgrounds, as they would still

be able to maintain familial and workplace ties. Diverse skills and perspectives, notably absent in our current political organizations, will become increasingly necessary if we are to overcome the challenges of living in this fast-paced, ever-changing world.

Deputy Cabinet Ministers

Normally, Public Representatives would resign from politics at the end of their five-year term. However, some may be asked by a Cabinet Minister to stay on and serve as one of their Deputy Cabinet Ministers.[4] Three or four Deputy Cabinet Ministers would normally assist each Cabinet Minister, depending on the responsibilities covered by the portfolio. The Deputy would serve for a maximum of three years in that position, at the end of which he or she would retire from politics, unless again chosen for higher office (such as to become a Cabinet Minister).

Deputy Cabinet Ministers would remain in their home Electoral Districts and would be responsible for helping their Minister perform his or her duties, such as communicating with other members of the Federal House of Representatives and drafting reports for discussion. As with the job of Public Representative, Deputy Cabinet Ministers would work part time, approximately 15 hours per week. In recognition of the extra work they would do, they would be paid a more generous honorarium than that received by the Public Representatives. They would work out of the same Electoral District office that the Public Representatives use, so they would have access to all the same communications systems.

Cabinet Ministers

The job of Cabinet Minister would be a full-time, salaried position, necessitating a move to Ottawa. While there, the Cabinet Minister would work with the other senior government officials at what could be the "nerve centre" for the federal government. This workplace would contain all the communications and information hook-ups necessary to maintain their networks across the country, as well as offices and resources for the various support staff and senior bureaucratic advisors.

A Cabinet Minister would serve a maximum of four years, after which he or she would retire from the government, unless again chosen for higher office (such as to become a Deputy Prime Minister). Along with being responsible for a portfolio, the Cabinet Minister would have the responsibility of replacing any of the Deputies as openings become available.

Once a Cabinet Minister retires or moves on to a higher office, the Prime Minister, assisted by the Deputy Prime Ministers and the retiring Minister, would choose one of the Deputy Cabinet Ministers to become the new Cabinet Minister. The new Minister would normally be one of the retiring Cabinet Minister's Deputies, but in unusual situations, a Deputy in another portfolio could be chosen for the post, especially if none of those in the current portfolio were able to move to Ottawa.

Deputy Prime Ministers

Two or three Deputy Prime Ministers would serve as assistants to the Prime Minister, serving for a maximum of four years. As veteran Deputies retire, replacements would be chosen by the Prime Minister from the ranks of the Cabinet Ministers. As with the Cabinet Ministers, they would work full time from Ottawa. At the end of their term, they would retire from the government, unless they are appointed to the post of Prime Minister.

Prime Minister

By the time a Canadian rises to the post of Prime Minister, he or she will normally have served at every level of the Federal House of Representatives and will probably have at least 12 years of experience (four as a Public Representative, two as a Deputy Cabinet Minister, three as a Cabinet Minister, and three as a Deputy Prime Minister). The process of continually choosing the most skilled individuals to advance to higher office would ensure that each Prime Minister would not only be extremely competent, but would also have an excellent understanding of how the political process works, coupled with a firm grounding in the real world of Canadian society. After serving for four years, the Prime Minister would retire, and one of the Deputy Prime Ministers (or Cabinet Ministers if no Deputy is willing or able to serve) would be chosen by the Federal House of Representatives by majority ballot as the successor.

A Non-partisan Government to Benefit Us All

Obviously, the model that I have presented is more conceptual than specific; a great deal of work would be required for us to hope to get such an auspicious project off the ground. I strongly believe, however, that we owe it to ourselves to make the effort. Instead of dividing us, our political system could be used to bring us together, to help us to overcome the many challenges that we will meet in the next millennium and beyond.

Such a shift in the way in which we govern ourselves would signal to the world, as well as to ourselves, that Canada is willing to take the necessary steps to mature into a strong, self-confident country that we all would feel proud to pass on to our children. It would say to everyone that we, as a society, are prepared to stand up and take control of our destiny, and accept the responsibilities which come with the privileges we gain for living in this beautiful land.

Notes

1. Most notably the poor and uneducated.
2. Perhaps to the consternation of our current political masters.
3. I would either abolish the Senate completely or change it into an advisory council made up of various experts from each province who would be appointed by the individual provinces and would serve in an advisory role only. They would not have any voting duties.
4. Note that this appointment could happen at any time during the Public Representative's five-year term, not just at the end.

Rules, Reforms, and Mandatory Community Work: The Get-Tough Plan for a Revitalized Canada

ANITA GIBBINGS

ANITA GIBBINGS

A resident of Swift Current, Saskatchewan, Anita is in the fourth year of the Bachelor of Commerce co-op program at Dalhousie University and also takes courses at Saint Mary's University. Anita has started her own business, Carpe Diem Opportunities Inc., which is a database service. She has taught English as a second language in Halifax and volunteered as an English-language tutor assisting immigrants. She is the former president of AIESEC Saint Mary's, an international students' organization, and has served on the Judicial Board of Dalhousie University. Anita enjoys numerous activities including rock climbing, Tai Chi, and yoga. She is the winner of several student entrepreneurial and marketing awards.

The first part of this essay provides three suggestions for improving the standard of living of Canadians: to increase the efficiency and effectiveness of the services offered by the government, to reduce the violence in society, and to enforce mandatory community involvement. The second part deals with a long-term plan to unify the country; moreover, some suggestions provide for the immediate improvement of relations between the Quebecois and the rest of the country.

To improve Canadians' standard of living the tax dollar must be spent efficiently and effectively so that more services can be provided for the same cost. Since the government cannot provide every service that Canadians want, the people should decide which services and other benefits that they want to pay for with their tax dollar. It must be kept in mind that people do not always know what is best for them and it is the government's job to ensure that every action will benefit Canadians in the long term. The government must concentrate on sustainable growth because it is better to have slower, steady growth than to deplete our resources and leave the next generation with a substantially lower standard of living. To find out what services Canadians want, each citizen could be mailed a form that would give a breakdown of how the government spends its money. Given a set budget based on the expected revenue, Canadians could choose the services that they want to see the government continue to provide. The government's reputation would improve if it listened more closely to the people whom it represents. In addition, this exercise would assist people to recognize that it is impossible to balance the budget without undesirable cuts in services offered and increased taxes.

Canadians perceive the government to waste tax money; to rectify this problem the attitude and culture within departments must change to focus on efficiency and effectiveness. To achieve this, the departments should be run more like a business that provides services to the paying customer, because Canadians pay through tax dollars. The people who know best how to reduce inefficiencies are the people who work in the departments. In order to get employees to make suggestions for increasing efficiency and effectiveness, they need to be rewarded for cost-cutting measures and finding innovative ways to do things better. Rewards should be given to department managers for being under budget. A large part of managers' salaries should be tied to their performance and measured on their ability to be under budget and keep the customers satisfied. Employees should be paid on a performance basis and bonuses paid for progressive ideas.

Two areas that need reform so that they can accomplish their purpose are the unemployment and welfare systems. To reduce the amount of abuse of the unemployment insurance system, an on-line service that required employers to post the names and social insurance numbers of every person who applied for a position would make it easy to prove whether someone is looking for a job. This could be available through the Internet so that employers could either go to their Canada Employment Centre or log on to the system directly (using their business number) from their office. This would eliminate the large number of people claiming unemployment insurance but not searching for a new job.

The welfare system does not improve Canadians' standard of living when the money is used to buy alcohol, lottery tickets, and cigarettes, often leaving children hungry. To stop some of these abuses, money could be provided in food and rent stamps. It would have to be impossible to turn these stamps into money so that they could not be sold on the black market. The person would be required to show several pieces of identification to use the stamp. Of course, some additional money must be provided; however, this would ensure that there is money for food.

To improve the standard of living, the government should concentrate on reducing violence in society. Security and peace are highly valued by Canadians and people do not want to follow the Americans in the trend towards rising violence. One of the major causes of this increase violence is the easy access to weapons. There is no reason to have a weapon, even for defence purposes, since it is rare that carrying a weapon will protect the anyone if attacked. There should be no licences for guns or knives; if hunters want a gun during the season, then one can be rented under very strict regulations. This requires a long process of eliminating guns by revoking all the licences and buying the guns from the owners, but nothing worth having is easily obtainable. With fewer weapons in Canada and a strong penalty for possession, there would be fewer murders, rapes, and other violent crimes. The Canadian borders would have to be controlled more strictly than they are now to slow the illegal import of guns into Canada. At the drive-across borders, security similar to that in airports is needed. Each piece of luggage needs to be run through a scanner and metal detector and each car thoroughly searched. This additional security, though costly and slow, would be worth the decrease in violence.

Standard of living is not defined by the amount of wealth per person but by the amount of happiness and fulfillment. Society could be greatly improved if there were more people involved in their communities and helping each other, especially those in need—the elderly, children in poverty, the mentally handicapped, and so forth. To make this mandatory, volunteer work would have to be organized in such a way that is appropriate for a free and democratic society. A system would be set up so that the individual chooses the kind of community work (within certain boundaries) and the time (although a certain number of hours over a certain period would be set). Individuals could choose to do their volunteer work overseas or in their own neighbourhoods. The government would also provide provisions for exemptions, excuses, and objective alternatives. Community service cannot tie up the lives of the individuals and the number of hours required would be flexible and kept at a fairly low minimum. But just imagine what a different place Canada would be if people over the age of 14 were to do five hours of community service every month: the elderly would no longer be lonely, people in hospitals would have visitors, the parks would be clean of garbage, playgrounds would be newly painted, children would have role models and build self-esteem, and the mentally or physically handicapped would lead fuller lives. Today, we are blind to addressable needs all around us but a community service model nurtured from childhood would open our eyes and our practical imaginations.

To enforce the community service it could be mandatory for students to complete a specified number of hours in order to qualify for a lower tuition rate. Students who do community service would pay tuition rates similar to what students pay now, while those who choose not to volunteer would pay double or triple the tuition. High school students who do no community service work would be required to pay tuition. For non-students, the incentive could be tax concessions or incentives. In addition to financial rewards, there should be recognition at a national level for outstanding contributions to society.

To unite the country, one must find what has caused the desire for separation and find a solution to achieve long-lasting unity. The main cause behind Quebec's desire for sovereignty is the fear of losing its identity in a mainly English-speaking country. Traditionally, Canadians have had a very weak Canadian identity since most citizens are not clear about what it means to be Canadian. In Canada, individuals are encouraged to promote and keep their own culture but this leaves many people unclear about what unifies everyone as Canadians. People need a common bond in order to feel as though they belong in the country. The Canadian identity cannot be built on cultural traditions without losing our multiculturalism; however, it can be built on common values. Because there are regional and cultural differences in such a large country, there needs to a stronger federal presence so that people will feel that they are Canadian before Maritimers, Westerners, Quebecois, or Ontarians.

To implement this solution, there first needs to be a consensus on what it means to be Canadian. The government should ask people what it means to be Canadian to determine our identity. During the next election, people could briefly write down what being a Canadian means to them or list their values. Canadians will most likely answer with things such as promoting peace, equality, multiculturalism, racial tolerance, security (social programs and health care), community involvement, environmental friendliness, and human rights. Canadians are known for our friendliness and our cultural understanding, especially when entertaining visitors to our country or travelling.

Second, it must be decided how to promote the Canadian identity. It will take years to change people's attitudes because long-ingrained beliefs about one's identity are difficult and slow to change. It is better to invest the time in a remedy than to ignore the underlying cause and cover up the problem. It is most effective to educate young people about what it means to be Canadian and have them grow up with the beliefs; therefore, the ideal method is to use the education system.

To unite the country and increase people's pride in being Canadian, students should learn more about each region. It would be good for the federal government to make a short film about each region so that students can see what it is really like. Also, experiences that bring young people from all across Canada together, such as visiting the Terry Fox Centre in Ottawa, should be promoted and increased. Even more effective is the Rotary Club's "Adventure in Citizenship," where students meet in Ottawa and spend a week learning about Canadian government and each of the different regions. Students should be exposed to films about different nationalities in Canada and what it means to them to come here and become citizens. Films are effective teaching tools because everyone gets the same message, and the impact of actual immigrants will have a lasting impression. The present education curriculum does not emphasize understanding different cultures, which is necessary for racial tolerance and multiculturalism. Students should learn more about countries on each continent from films and, if possible, natives of that country.

One of the best ways to build Canadian pride, and therefore unify the country, is to conduct international exchanges. Someone who travels to another country comes back with a much clearer idea of what it means to be Canadian and an appreciation of this country, which they share with their friends, family, colleagues at work, and fellow students. Young people need more assistance to gain international experience. Canada does not emphasize international experience or have as many people travelling as do the United States, Australia, and Europe. Germany has a policy to ensure that one out of three students participates in some form of international exchange, whether it is an internship or a study program. When one visits Germany, people's pride in being German is immediately obvious. International exchanges can build the number of business contacts and give Canadians experience in cultural understanding and language skills that are invaluable in business ventures in other countries. The Canadian market is small and, to foster growth in the economy, Canadian businesses need to export.

The above suggestion is a long-term solution to unify the country; however, more immediate results are needed to avoid another referendum. Canada cannot give Quebec any special rights, because if one group receives them the other will also demand them; this contradicts the value of equality. The Prime Minister must firmly maintain that all Canadians are equal and that no group can be given special rights and privileges; otherwise, racial tensions will increase. Quebec can be guaranteed that any legislation that measurably harms the French culture will be prevented from becoming law. It should be emphasized that French and English Canadians can work together to improve our standard of living and that we can both win by staying together. The problem is that there are anger and hostility because neither group feels as if its views are held as important or are understood. Both sides should take turns listening without interrupting until both parties feel understood. Once they feel understood, they can work on solutions that will benefit both. Canadians will be hypocritical if they suggest that countries such as South Africa, Bosnia, and Israel live peacefully with their many distinct cultures, religions, and beliefs when as Canadians we cannot, even though our differences are comparatively insignificant.

To bring about unity we need a strong leader in a Prime Minister, a person who believes in Canada and is proud to be Canadian to lead and inspire Canadians with his or her vision. We cannot have a leader who refuses to take a stance on any issue for fear that it will not be universally popular. The Prime Minister must be committed to looking for a solution so both French and English Canadians can win. The concerns of Quebec cannot be disregarded, because without a solution, the separatist movement will be fuelled by the government's inability to address Quebecois needs and the separatists will win the next referendum.

As we move into the 21st century, there are many challenges in a world that is becoming more and more complex. The Prime Minister must listen to the people he or she governs because it is they who will come up with the solutions to improve Canada. The Prime Minister must simply provide the leadership qualities to lead Canadians through the changes. The potential for Canada lies not with the Prime Minister but in the way that Prime Minister harnesses the genius of the people.

The Rise of
the Canadian Phoenix

PARKER MITCHELL

PARKER MITCHELL

Parker is entering the third year of the mechanical engineering program at the University of Waterloo. A resident of Westmount, Quebec, Parker represented the University of Waterloo at the Léger Cup debating competition. He is director of the Engineering Communications Club at Waterloo and serves on the board of directors of the Stanford Fleming Foundation, a non-profit organization dedicated to excellence in engineering. He was founder and editor of the *Midnight Sun Newsletter*, a monthly publication covering the Midnight Sun solar-powered race car. Parker is a member of the varsity rugby team and has competed in the Canadian National Championships of sailing.

"Man is by nature a political animal" – Aristotle, *Politics*

The very essence of the Canadian way of life—a strong social security system, universal health care, readily available education—is under fire. From all corners of the country new assailants enter the fray, voicing demands for privatization. People from Newfoundland to British Columbia are rallying to cries of decentralization or even separation. And all this in a country that, a scant four years ago, was voted the best country in the world in which to live. Somewhere along the line, the system has broken down; right now we're witnessing a desperate attempt to grease the bearings and get back on track. Unfortunately, the machinery within which our system operates is itself obsolete and in need of replacement. What follows is an outline of the system I would implement, were I Prime Minister, to lay the foundation needed to improve the average Canadian's quality of living.

The ultimate goal of any democratic system of government is to improve every citizen's standard of living; to do so, such a system must not only attract people whose aims match those of the citizens, but it must also retain its accountability to those citizens. Unfortunately, ordinary Canadians are hamstrung by an archaic electoral system that hands unchecked power to a limited few whose concern for that power outweighs their sense of civic responsibility. The current system has three major flaws, and their resolution precedes any improvement in our quality of living:

1) Government is not truly accountable to the people.
2) The transition between governments is rough.
3) Power is concentrated in the hands of a select few.

In the Canadian system, a majority party has the equivalent of a five-year dictatorship during which it can pass almost any legislation. This is clearly contrary to the idea that government must be accountable to the people in order to maintain an equilibrium between its actions and the people's views. Yet, no matter how unpopular a ruling party is, the public is left with no recourse until the next election. This second factor introduces a rough transition between governments, since the newly elected party wastes important time undoing its predecessor's policies.

Third, and most important, however, this lack of accountability can lead to an abuse of power. There is a well-known maxim that states: "Power corrupts, and absolute power corrupts absolutely." Canada is no exception. The existence of this widespread self-interest is in itself probably the single, most destructive factor in politics. For when the leaders who control our future no longer have our best interests in mind, progress cannot help but be limited. In addition, any leaders who manage to maintain their sense of righteousness are nonetheless restricted by their corruptible colleagues. Therefore, any new system must both attract and retain persons of integrity who are politically and socially altruistic, and provide a framework within which they can actualize their ideas.

If it is power that corrupts, then the way to prevent corruption is to dilute the power held by the few and spread it amongst the many. The dilution of power that accompanies the truly representative government outlined below will change the face of politics; it will starve the self-serving representative out of office by eliminating the power upon which corruption feeds. However, to do so we must take advantage of the technology that is with us every day. No longer can we afford to abide by rules that were initiated by an English feudal monarchy. We must burn the very idea that has prevailed throughout modern Western thought—the idea that the government's functions must be performed by a select few—and return to ancient Athens, where democracy took root. At its inset, democracy meant that every Athenian (albeit only the males) had the right to vote on every bill. The ever-growing population has since made this an impossible ideal, but with the advent of computers and mass communications, it is again feasible. With this in mind, the essential tenet for diluting the power base and returning to a true democracy is to grant every Canadian the opportunity to vote on every bill. The way it would work follows.

Structure

The basic element of the system would be the "Camp," a group of between 25 and 40 eligible voters who would meet once a year to elect a representative—the custodian of their votes. Once every week or two, the representatives of each "District" (comprising 20 to 25 Camps) would meet to discuss and vote on any legislation before them. The entire system would be computerized using a system similar to the Internet that provides legislation and other relevant information. Each representative would be issued a special "voting card," which would be used to cast the number of votes equal to the citizens represented by that person.

However, eligible Canadians would also be issued personal voting cards. If they felt that their views were not adequately represented, they would be free to attend the District meeting and vote. By voting, they would alert the computer that, for that particular bill only, they had chosen not to allow their representative to vote on their behalf, and so the representative's card would count one fewer people.

The penultimate level would be "Regions": 300 spread across Canada, consisting of 120 Districts, each of which elects one representative. The Regions are not an integral part of the system; they would meet infrequently but would serve as intermediary between the Districts and the government, as well as the two functions mentioned below.

The government would still consist of two legislative bodies, but both would have the ability to introduce legislation. The House of Socrates would resemble the House of Commons of today; it would be elected by the general population every four years. Representatives to the House of Plato, which would resemble the current Senate, would be chosen in an annual election by the 120 representatives of each Region.

Legislation

In most cases, each bill would be introduced and passed by the House of Socrates. Once this had occurred, the bill would be earmarked for one of the two remaining levels: the House of Plato or the districts. Both these levels keep the government accountable to the people; in order for legislation to become law, it must be passed by the populace. However, although every bill is available to be voted on at the District level, the sheer logistics preclude such lofty ideals. Thus, when a District chooses not to vote on a particular issue, its votes are passed to its representative to the House of Plato. For example, if half the Districts of a particular Region vote on a certain bill, then those votes (those of the eligible voters that the Districts represent) would be tallied by computer and stored. Then, the Plato representative's vote would count for the people from that Region's remaining districts.

This would allow all Canadians the opportunity to vote on any bill they choose. Frequently, they may choose to forgo that right and give it to their Camp representative. If that representative at the District level did not vote, then that person's vote, along with all the others from the District, would be given to the Plato representative to cast. So, for every vote, the totals should be equal to the entire voting population.

Finally, on rare occasions, there would also be legislation that could be initiated by the general populace. A concerned citizen could table a bill at the District level, which would vote on sending it up to the regional level. Once there, the Region would vote on whether it should continue to the House of Plato. If the House of Plato approved it, it would follow the same procedure as a bill that had been passed by the House of Socrates, except that it would have to be approved (by the Districts) by a majority of 66 percent prior to becoming law. This is the only case when the House of Plato can introduce legislation, but it is nonetheless essential, because it allows the people, in extenuating circumstances, to force the government to adopt various policies, although they require a broad consensus to do so.

Advantages

I have already delineated the problems with the current government—a lack of true representation, a rough transition from one government to another, the abuse of power—and shown that attracting trustworthy citizens to serve their country and providing a framework to aid them would benefit us immensely. We will now proceed to show how this plan accomplishes those aims.

While this system is in no way a panacea, it would, in one stroke, make government accountable to the people, smooth over the transition between governments, and prevent corruption by diluting the power base. Moreover, it does so in a way that allows the concerned citizen to participate actively in the democratic process while it minimizes the disruption to the daily routine of indifferent persons. Finally, it would also unite Canadians across the country both by involving them directly in the democratic process and by reinstating the sense of community that has fallen victim to our expanding metropolises.

Once this system were in place, the only successful legislation would be that sanctioned by the public. No longer could a politician or political party pass legislation that benefits the few, for neither would have the final say any longer. This would result in a more stable political system that smoothes the transition between governments. Though the emphasis would shift from the political party to the populace, there would still be a multi-party system that provided alternative political views to an electorate. The difference is that in order for the government to implement those ideas, it must convince the public of their validity. Not only would this open up hitherto closed governmental doors, but also any successful legislation would be instituted much more rapidly, because the public would be in accord with the policies.

The crucial improvement in this system is the method in which power would be reduced. No longer could a politician be influenced by self-interest or special interest groups—it is significantly harder to wine and dine a nation than an individual! This dilution of power would gradually eliminate the power-hungry influence peddler from the realm of politics, and open the door for more civic-minded individuals. Moreover, it would provide the framework that allows those individuals to voice their ideas for improving the country directly to the populace and those ideas supported by the people to be implemented. It would allow those people who are concerned a chance to participate in the process, while it would barely affect

those who are not. The final result is that every citizen would benefit from a civic-minded government that administers national affairs
while maintaining the right to step in at any time and control unpopular legislation.

Other Advantages

There is also an intangible benefit from this plan that was mentioned
briefly, namely the sense of unity that this system would help foster at
both the community level and national level. Be it running in the
Terry Fox run, playing hockey at the local outdoor rink, or cheering
for our athletes at the Olympics, there is nothing so unifying as know-
ing that someone, somewhere within this huge nation, is participating
in an identical activity. Allowing everyone to vote on issues would
instill a feeling of collective unity, linking fellow voters from St. John's
to Victoria. No longer could citizens complain that they were
deceived by election promises or manipulated by the media; if they
have a gripe, they would now have a forum in which to air their views
and have an influence, albeit small, over policy.

With the advent of technology, one problem that has wrought
havoc across the First World is the lack of community spirit that per-
vades our cities. While technology has undoubtedly increased our
independence, that very fact has contributed to our isolation. Gone
are the days when neighbours would look out for one another, when
Samaritans would stop to help people. Our dependence on technology has separated us from our community habits, and it is high time
those habits were restored. Rather than being cloistered inside, mes-
merized by a television, people would feel a sense of belonging if they
participated actively in their communities. The level of crime and feeling of collective helplessness would decrease if only people retained
their community values and looked out for their neighbour.

This system would help foster that sense of community by bringing people together at a local level. The small size of the Camps are
structured to allow personal interaction, to allow the elected representative to know each of the roughly 30 "constituents" personally.
Moreover, these neighbours would meet together annually to elect

their representative. From these meetings the bond of common geography would gradually strengthen into a community.

Growing from these neighbourhoods, the Districts would provide an opportunity for like-minded people in a local area to congregate and exchange ideas. Ideally, these Districts would help or eventually supplant the municipal level of government, eliminating some of the redundancy that would otherwise occur. By bringing people together, this system would lay the foundation of community that a strong sense of nationhood needs in order to flourish.

Conclusion

As Prime Minister, I would find it ironic to dismantle the very institution that elected me. It is perhaps even dangerous to question the system that has afforded the most freedom in the political world thus far. But it is even more dangerous for Canadians to sit back passively and allow the status quo to remain unchallenged, for if we wait long enough, we may no longer have a country to save. Systems themselves are fallible, and what yesterday was satisfactory, today must be replaced. Since the demise of the ancient Greeks we have been living in a state of adultered democracy, which, given the advent of telecommunications and the Internet, is no longer necessary. The possibility once again exists to exercise a rule of the people, by the people, and for the people, as Democritus truly intended.

And so, if I were Prime Minister, I would propose this plan. I would recommend it to the people, I would explain it to them, and I would create the infrastructure necessary to implement it. And if, in a referendum, I were given a resounding mandate to proceed, I would implement it. A new generation of citizens would rise out of the ashes of the very system that was dismantled and burnt, spreading their wings like the legendary Phoenix, to help lead this country towards prosperity. But without the fire, the Phoenix cannot rise; without the demise of the current system, these people cannot step forward. Because, in the end, it is the citizens who make Canada the wonderful country it is.

Restoring Canada's Prosperity and Canadians' Faith in Democracy: A Plan for Reform

LANCE LEHMAN

LANCE LEHMAN

Lance is in the second of a three-year program at Osgoode Law School at York University and holds a Bachelor of Arts in Canadian Studies from the University of Guelph, where he graduated with distinction. He works part-time as a case worker for the Community and Legal Aid Services Program, providing legal counselling to legal aid recipients. While at the University of Guelph, he served as a College of Arts Senator and helped draft a new constitutional section to facilitate electoral reform. A former softball coach, Lance is active in baseball and volleyball and his interests include violin, reading, and politics.

Canada is a land of magnificent beauty and abundant natural resources. It is a nation whose people are among the most healthy and well educated in the world. Canadians are global leaders in the pharmaceutical industry, computer software development, and tele-communications technology. Yet Canada is a country facing profound problems. Canadians are discouraged and pessimistic in the face of chronically high rates of unemployment, spiralling government debt, and a tax burden that seems to grow exponentially. Destructive government policies such as the National Energy Program have fostered resentment in the Western provinces towards the Central provinces while a full-fledged separatist movement in Quebec is poised to tear the country apart. For too long, Canada's leaders have floundered in a sea of indecision and political cowardice, haphazardly trying to hold the country together by imposing an unwanted and artificial culture in the form of official bilingualism and multiculturalism while mortgaging our country's future and allowing its problems to compound to the point that we now stand at the brink of ruin.

As Prime Minister of Canada, I would embark upon a program of rational and innovative solutions to address the country's most threatening problems. Essentially, these problems can be categorized as relating primarily to either national unity or to living standards. I shall therefore discuss my proposals according to that categorization.

Developing National Unity

Institutional Reform

Underlying Canada's lack of national unity is the fact that Canada's current federal structure is designed in such a way that is politically advantageous for the federal and provincial governments to blame Canada's problems on one another. This contributes to a feeling among the population that governments are inept and corrupt, and that each province, or at least each region of the country, is in competition with the other provinces or regions. As Prime Minister of Canada, I would endeavour to reform the structure of the federal government so as to reduce the tendency among our governments to shift blame.

Specifically, I propose that the federal Cabinet be restructured to include one delegate from each of the 10 provincial governments in addition to up to 10 ministers selected by the Prime Minister from the House of Commons. In this way, provincial governments would be strongly discouraged from attacking the federal government for purely political reasons because to do so could be seen as criticizing their own delegates. At the same time, provincial interests would be represented at the federal level, eliminating the need to reform the Senate. In fact, the Senate could then be abolished.

A second institutional reform that I would initiate in order to restore Canadians' faith in their leaders, and therefore in their country, would be to implement a system whereby the federal and provincial Cabinets would be proportionally representative of the legislatures. That is to say, Cabinet positions at both the federal and provincial levels would be appointed to each party in proportion to the number of seats that the party holds in the respective legislatures. The adversarial system of government encourages political posturing and unprincipled criticizing. By implementing this reform, compromise and consensus would be encouraged, reducing the purely political grandstanding that has earned our politicians the contempt of the nation. At the same time, the "first past the post" system of deciding elections would be maintained, avoiding short-lived, Italian-style coalition governments.

I believe that these two reforms would go a long way towards ending the political manoeuvring by competing governments and parties that interferes with the business of the nation and that so disgusts Canadians. Thus, Canadians would come to believe in the efficacy of their governmental structures and perhaps to see the good intentions that drive most politicians. However, mere structural reform is not sufficient to develop the sense of national unity that is so needed in Canada today. In order to achieve that lofty goal, other innovative policies must also be initiated.

Developing Good Citizenship

Individual Canadians derive a great deal of benefit from their citizenship. Canadians receive government-funded health care, subsidized education, and a social safety net that guarantees no Canadian will ever be destitute. I believe that it is not unreasonable to require that Canadians give something back in the form of public service. I therefore propose that at age 18, all Canadians, with very few exceptions, be required to participate in some program of national service for a period of four months. This could include military service, but it could also take the form of working in national parks or in other worthwhile projects. While employed in such projects, the government would be responsible to feed and house the youths, but in terms of monetary reward, only a small stipend ought to be extended.

I believe that a project of this nature would engender a sense of common experience among Canadians that is lacking because of Canada's vast and varied geography. This would especially be true if the system were structured so as to encourage Canadian youths to perform their public service in a different part of the country from where they live. The system would foster national pride and strong work ethics and would serve the country's physical well-being.

Just as a sense of common experience would help to foster national unity, so too would a sense of common history. Unfortunately, most Canadians are largely unaware of this country's rich and fascinating history. Too many Canadians identify history as the history of their ancestral origin. While there is nothing wrong with being aware of one's individual heritage, it is also important that each of us be aware of our collective heritage. To that end, as Prime Minister I would embark upon a program of national history education in our schools and our public media. I would also terminate all government-sponsored multiculturalism programs and would offer bilingual services only where the public wants them.

Improving Living Standards

Taxation and Fiscal Reform

Arguably, the most important aspect of that which we term "living standards" is the productivity of our economy. Most Canadians agree that living standards are improved when the economy grows, producing jobs and greater disposable incomes. Therefore, with the goal

of encouraging economic activity, as Prime Minister I would restructure our taxation system so as to maximize incentives to individuals
and businesses to create wealth and to keep it in Canada.

I would begin by replacing the current progressive personal taxation system with a "flat tax" of 25 percent on all earnings above the
basic personal deduction. With a very few exceptions that I will discuss shortly, all personal deductions and tax shelters would be eliminated so as to allow for this lower tax rate without completely
destroying the federal income tax base. Such a system would be eminently more fair than the current structure; its simplicity would save
time and money in accounting and auditing costs and it would help
to restore an incentive for individuals to work.

Second, I would end all government subsidies to private businesses and government involvement in "mega-projects" such as the
Hibernia project. Government subsidies and mega-projects merely
encourage inefficiency and perpetuate the existence of industries that
would not otherwise be viable. In addition, I would seek to privatize
any government industry that could be more efficiently handled by
the private sector, including, possibly, the CBC, electricity production
and delivery, infrastructure maintenance, liquor distribution, and
prisons. The massive amounts of money currently involved in such
endeavours would be much better invested in education and training
for workers or in debt retirement.

As Prime Minister of Canada, I would create an economic environment that encourages investment by committing the government
to achieve and maintain a balanced budget, while developing an effective infrastructure and keeping taxes at a reasonable level. I would
encourage businesses to invest in Canada by allowing them to deduct
in one year the cost of any capital investments made in Canada, rather
than having to depreciate the investments over several years. While I
would lower the corporate tax rate, I would also reduce the extent to
which corporations can deduct previous years' losses from the current
year's income so as to discourage foolish investments. Finally, I would
work to eliminate all interprovincial trade barriers. It is preposterous
that, in many cases, it is easier for Canadian businesses to sell their
products in a foreign market than to sell them in a neighbouring
province.

As previously mentioned, I believe that most personal deductions should be eliminated in order to accommodate the introduction of a flat tax rate. However, in order to foster economic activity and desirable social trends, I would continue to allow certain deductions such as those for contributions to RRSPs. Too many Canadians have become dependent on government support in recent decades. It is incumbent upon the government to reverse this trend and encourage people to take responsibility for themselves. I would also introduce a deduction for interest paid on a mortgage of a principle residence. The government of Canada should strive to encourage Canadians to be homeowners because this serves as a means of saving, reducing the likelihood that the individual in question will depend on government help later in life. Finally, I would continue to allow a tax deduction for childcare expenses and I would introduce a new tax deduction equivalent to the cost of putting a child in day care for parents who choose to stay home with their children. Raising healthy and responsible children is perhaps the most important task an individual in our society can undertake, yet our present tax structure discourages parents from caring for their own children.

Welfare and Unemployment Insurance Reform

Our social safety net is in dire need of repair. The current welfare and unemployment insurance systems provide virtually no incentives to individuals to seek permanent solutions to their inability to find work or to improve their education. In order to qualify for long-term welfare support, individuals other than those caring for small children and those who are handicapped ought to be required to improve their education or to participate in a work-training program. This concept, popularly referred to as "workfare," could be run by expanding private-sector industries; the business involved would be permitted to deduct twice the cost of employing the welfare recipient from its net income for the duration of the workfare program. Of course, the businesses would be approved by the government and only those businesses that retained a high percentage of workfare participants after the end of training would be repeatedly approved for the program. In this way, government would be relieved of the cost of supporting these welfare recipients, the recipients would continue to receive an income and training, and the businesses involved would be able to recruit and train new employees at a very low cost.

The reforms that are needed to correct the problems associated with the current unemployment insurance system are basically quite simple. First, there must be a limit placed on the number of times within an individual's working life that person may receive unemployment insurance. This would prevent the abuse that occurs when employers engage workers only so long as it takes to qualify for unemployment insurance and then simply lay the employees off until the insurance runs out. Admittedly, such a strict rule would unfairly prevent some people who are, by no fault of their own, unfortunate enough to require support several times during their working lives. However, the existence of short-term welfare and private unemployment insurance would compensate for these minor injustices.

The second reform that must be implemented to eliminate the incentive-killing nature of the present unemployment insurance regime is to remove its applicability to those who work in depressed industries or areas of the country and who refuse to relocate or to change industries. Critics of this proposal will argue that it amounts to forced relocation of citizens, violating the Canadian Charter of Rights, but this is an invalid criticism. In implementing such a reform, the government would not be forcibly relocating anyone, but merely stating society's unwillingness to blindly support those who are unwilling to help themselves.

Public Education and Justice Reform

While it is obviously extremely important, economic prosperity is not the only measure of a country's standard of living. As Prime Minister of Canada, I would seek to improve Canadians' standard of living in many ways. I would introduce basic training in family finance and childcare skills for all high school students, so as to encourage further individual responsibility and independence. I would also encourage healthy lifestyles and preventive health care by introducing nutrition classes in high schools and imposing additional taxes on tobacco and alcohol products. Furthermore, I would seek to reform our justice system.

Generally, our police forces and courts work extremely well, considering the existing framework of the criminal justice system. In many criminal cases justice is done. Unfortunately, justice is often not seen to be done because of the inability of the media to present all of the information related to a single case to the public. More disturbing is the fact that in some cases, the police and courts are unable to do justice because the current system of criminal law stipulates maximum sentences rather than minimum sentences.

As Prime Minister of Canada, I would initiate a pilot program of electing lower court judges by popular vote. This would allow the public to feel that it has a direct hand in protecting itself from criminal elements. Once elected, no judge would stand for re-election, eliminating the risk that judges might be tempted to do injustices so as to retain their position. I would also encourage courts to allow their proceedings to be televised so that the public could watch its justice system at work.

As a final reform to the justice system, I would amend the Criminal Code so as to impose a rebuttable presumption of "dangerous offender status" on all persons convicted of a sexual or extremely violent offence. Thus, unless the convicted person could prove that he or she was not a continuing risk to society, that person would be incarcerated indefinitely. I believe that these reforms would make Canadian society safer and thereby improve the standard of living.

Conclusion

Many of the reforms that I have proposed herein will be extremely difficult to implement without the cooperation of governments, business, and the public, but they are workable solutions to many of Canada's problems. To believe, however, that even these fundamental changes will forever quell Quebec separatism and completely unify the country is foolhardy. The Quebec separatist movement is an irrational movement driven only by emotion. That said, the reforms that I have proposed are in the interests of all Canadians and would help to prevent the Quebec separatists from gaining support among those Quebecois who do not seek an independant state for its own sake.

I am grateful to have had this opportunity to share my views on the future of our country and I hope sincerely that my thoughts will contribute in some way to making Canada a better place for the next generation of Canadians.

Won't You Be My Neighbour? A New Paradigm for the Canadian Community

CATHERINE CONNORS

CATHERINE CONNORS

Catherine is a political science major at Simon Fraser University in Burnaby, British Columbia. She is a former vice-president of academic affairs for the school's political science student union and a former student representative on the undergraduate curriculum committee of the political science department. Catherine was also vice-president of the school's United Nations Club and coordinator of the 1996–97 Model United Nations Team. She is an executive member of the Canadian Institute of International Affairs and a volunteer at the Vancouver Children's Festival.

When I was about four or five years old, one of my central concerns was figuring out who I was and where I came from. I received many vague and confusing answers to my questions: apparently, I came from God, but Nanny came from Scotland and Daddy came from a place called Ontario. I knew that I was Daddy's girl, so it followed that we would come from the same place. But Nanny was old and the closest thing to God that I could fathom. So I decided that Scotland was somewhere close to heaven and that Ontario was somewhere in between.

My home, I was told, was Canada. My home, according to my mother, was not necessarily where I came from, but rather where I was supposed to be. I knew that my home was something that included more than just my house—I supposed that it included my yard, and my street, and the park, and the corner store, and so on. From this, I determined that Canada was the neighbourhood in which I lived, and that it extended from Dogwood Crescent, where our house was located, to the approximate location of my playschool. This conception of Canada stayed with me until a well-meaning primary school teacher showed me a globe and explained that my neighbourhood was part of Canada. She also pointed out Ontario and Scotland.

I was horrified. I hadn't realized God lived so very far away.

As an adult, I've returned to my childhood conception of Canada as a neighbourhood. It was, I've decided, not so far from the truth. Like my childhood neighbourhood, Canada is composed of a wide variety of people from a wide variety of places. Furthermore, the citizens of Canada, like the residents of my neighbourhood, are not bound most centrally by common blood or heritage (although that was sometimes the case), but by the fact that we share a home. A home that we love. Regardless of where any of us might be from, Canada is where each of us is supposed to be. As Prime Minister, my primary objectives would be to promote the idea of the Canadian neighbourhood and, through reforms in Canada's electoral, governmental, and social systems, to strengthen that neighbourhood.

Canada is currently experiencing a profound malaise—economic, social, and political. Our debt and deficit seem to have spiralled out of control. Unemployment rates have risen as the standard of living for most Canadians has fallen. We distrust our politicians and our political system. And we have become uncertain of our identities and our loyalties. Am I Canadian, English-Canadian, or British Columbian? Are those identities exclusive to one another—or do they mean the same thing?

What has happened to our neighbourhood? Is this where we're supposed to be?

Canada, I would argue, is on the verge of maturity. It has a developmental dilemma and must determine whether it should adhere to the external influences (its colonial upbringing, its elder American cousin) of its youth, or grow in its own national "adult" direction. Canada's current malaise is, in large part, a symptom of its growing pains, and only by launching itself wholeheartedly into the spirit of growth and change will Canada blossom into the national neighbourhood that it can be. I'm not Mister Rogers, but I do believe that the principles of good neighbourhood[1] can be applied to both the problem of national unity and the problem of improving living standards.

National Unity

National unity rests as much in public confidence in the national political system as it does in national symbolism and identity. Members of any community, be it neighbourhood or nation, identify with that community not only because they reside within it, but also because they participate in it and identify with it. If members of a community become estranged from the development and maintenance of that community, they become alienated from the community itself; cynicism grows and bonds weaken. This is precisely what has happened in Canada. The various constituent, provincial, and regional members of the Canadian neighbourhood have become estranged as the national government has become increasingly separated from the Canadian public. Ottawa seems a foreign entity run by foreigners, an entity that is increasingly irrelevant to the average Canadian.

The primary source of this problem is the seeming lack of representation provided by the federal government, a problem that is underscored by Canadians' disparate perceptions of that government. When asked whom the federal government represents, Westerners say "central Canadian interests," the Quebecois say "English-Canadian interests," and many others say "special interests"; one would be hard-pressed to find a group in Canada that fully identifies with the federal government and feels that it is represented by it. This is a serious problem; our lack of confidence in our national governing institution erodes our identification of ourselves as a nation. Alienation increases and the seeds of discord are sown amongst the increasingly estranged members of the community.

So what is the solution?

A popular proposal is increased decentralization—each province should manage its own household and take care of its own yard. There seems to be a certain reasonableness to this proposal—if the federal government does not adequately represent the interests of localized communities, then more responsibility should be given to the provincial governments that do seem to represent those interests. We would, it can be argued, have less to bicker about if we were more in charge of our own affairs; there would be fewer accusations of certain provinces having more favoured status, and thus there would be less resentment and suspicion among the provinces. We'd all live together peacefully.

Maybe. Maybe not. What would, however, be guaranteed in a decentralized system of provincial isolationism would be diminished national identity and possibly entrenched differences and tensions. Our neighbours would become strangers to be regarded with suspicion, and developing and promoting national identity would become almost insurmountable tasks if most interests were localized. We would, quite simply, lose our common ground and with it, our sense of community. We might live peacefully, but we would certainly live in isolation.

There is another alternative, one that strikes a balance between the benefits of decentralizing responsibilities and centralizing identity and loyalty. A program of modified decentralization that decentralizes significant jurisdictional authority while restructuring national political activity to make it more inclusive would accord each province and region greater jurisdictional autonomy at the same time it centralizes identity and national focus. The transfer of powers would be accomplished through constitutional amendment; restructuring national political activity could be achieved by amending elements of the national electoral system and the parliamentary system.

An in-depth exploration of jurisdictions to be transferred is beyond the scope of this proposal. It must be noted, however, that the decentralization of powers would be negotiated between the federal government and the provinces, with all amendments applied equally to all provinces. The jurisdiction of the federal government over defence, foreign policy, taxation and revenue, financial institutions, currency and common debt, and customs and tariffs, would, however, be non-negotiable.

The amendments to the electoral and parliamentary systems do bear in-depth explication. Canada employs a single-member plurality—or "first past the post"—electoral system. There are two important flaws with this system. First, the candidate who is first past the post in a given riding is not necessarily supported by a majority of constituents; often, the winning candidate is only supported by a minority of voters. The preferences of the majority, in this case, are not represented; public cynicism towards elected "representatives" is therefore guaranteed in the single-member plurality system. Second, this lack of translated preferences occurs on a much larger scale in the determination of government by number of seats. A party, like individual candidates, may win a minority of the popular vote but still gain a majority of seats. While this facilitates the formation of majority governments that are arguably more efficient at governing, it does not reflect the will of the voting public. "Federal representation" becomes an oxymoron.

This creates a gulf between the public and government—and, as argued above, a public that feels that its interests are not reflected or represented by its national government is more likely to identify with that which is more immediate and tangible—one's province, region, or ethnicity. The solution is twofold. First, the electoral system must be reformed in such a way as to translate voter preferences better into electoral results and thus ensure better representation. Second, the current parliamentary system and "chain of command" must be readjusted to facilitate citizen involvement in government.

In the first case, the *Electoral Act* could simply be amended to utilize a proportionally representative system of election. In the so-called "list system," parties provide lists of candidates in each province and are accorded seats according to the percentage of the vote that they receive. There are a number of advantages to this system; most important, it accurately translates voter preferences into political results and thus facilitates a truly representative government. It also facilitates the involvement of greater variety of minor parties, thereby allowing the electorate greater choice.[2]

There is a variety of criticisms that can be made in response to this system. For example, it has been argued that the proportionally representative system would, by allowing the clear articulation of a variety of preferences, draw more attention to the differences that exist amongst groups in Canada, thereby aggravating existing tensions.[3] This, however, disregards the tensions that are aggravated when differing opinions and preferences are not represented or articulated. Another argument holds that the relationship between the constituent and the member of Parliament would become distended in a proportionally representative system. That relationship, however, is already strained by the existing lack of direct contact between constituents and members of Parliament and the aforementioned tensions created by the lack of translated voter preference.

Arguments and counter-arguments aside, it must be acknowledged that this system is not a perfect system, only a superior one. The second part of my proposal is designed to address some of the potential drawbacks of the proportionally representative system while reforming the existing parliamentary system. I would restructure the parliamentary system by establishing Constituency Associations in each constituency[4] and eliminating the existing Senate.

Each constituency would have an association of members from that community who would meet regularly to analyze and discuss proposed federal legislation. These Association representatives would be selected randomly from the lists of eligible voters (similar to the jury system) and would serve a one-year, fully paid term.[5] They would have access to governmental resources (legal, advisory) and would formulate constituency positions on all relevant issues. The constituency member of Parliament would, in all matters of legislation, be advised of the constituency position and (in most cases) act accordingly, directly representing the constituency interests in government.

The number of constituencies in the country would be reduced by half while maintaining the same formula of distribution (thus, for example, New Brunswick's 10 seats would be reduced to five). The addition of a new stratum of government created by the implementation of Constituency Associations justifies this reduction: the responsibilities of representation and communication would not fall to an individual member of Parliament, but would be shared by that member and the constituency association.

The Constituency Associations would also function as community senates. Once legislation had been debated in the House of Commons and had passed on to the reading stages, it would be returned to the Constituency Associations for review and debate—in short, the Constituency Associations would function as the "sober second thought" that is supposed to be the Senate's function now. The Senate could, therefore, be abolished. Legislation would require majority approval of the Constituency Associations as well approval from the House. Stalemated issues would go to referendum.

There are two potential difficulties with the above arrangement. The first is the possible eradication of the need for parties. While many might applaud this, it remains that the functioning of government would become exceptionally tedious and inefficient with a large group of independent, constituency-advised members of Parliament working at cross-purposes. It is further difficult to imagine how government might be organized (selection of Prime Minister and Cabinet, for example) amongst wholly independent members. To circumvent these difficulties, the Constituency Association and party systems would have to be made compatible.

Parties would run for election in federal races in the proportionally representative system as described above; for this they would create lists of candidates for each province. They would also be required to provide a clear platform of intended action if elected. If that party were to win with a majority of the popular vote, it would be legally bound to that platform—that is to say, all members of that party would be required to hold to party position on issues relating to that platform. On all other issues, they could vote according to their constituency position. All other members of Parliament could vote according to their constituency position. In the case of minority governments (which occur often in proportionally representative systems), in which no party has a clear mandate, members of Parliament could choose between constituency positions and party position. Theoretically, this would force them to exercise caution in decision-making—a member with a record of continually rejecting Constituency Association positions would not be popular with the electorate—while at the same time allowing some freedom to exercise political judgement.

The second argument that might be raised against such a system concerns the problems of capability and efficiency. It could be argued that a) the average citizen is not capable of making informed, rational decisions on policy and legislation; and b) that even if the average citizen were capable, associations of such citizens would be incapable of reaching any sort of consensus. Furthermore, it might be argued, there would invariably be such disparate opinion emerging from these Constituency Associations that no government could act upon their advice.

There are a couple of responses to the above. First, this argument underestimates and ignores the capabilities of Canadian citizens. If a used car salesman can be a member of Parliament, it is reasonable to assume that a tradesperson or teacher could also participate productively in national decision-making. The principle of democracy is based on the assumption that citizens are capable of participating in government and that the best society is one in which citizens have the opportunity to participate. Lest we entertain the possibility that public activity is an enterprise to be reserved for an elite few, and in doing so negate the principles of democracy, it must be assumed that most Canadians have the tools with which to participate in public life. Those tools would be supplemented (as they are for members of Parliament) by bureaucratic resources (that is, legal and technical advice).

As to the problem of inefficiency, it must first be stated that issues that trigger widespread public disagreement demand to be treated as slowly and carefully as possible. The good of society should never take a backseat to expediency. That said, the above-described provisions for independent decision-making would be retained to allow for political direction and leadership when needed. Constituency Associations would not dictate federal direction; they would merely contribute to the determination of that direction.

With a reformed electoral system, government would be made to be more clearly representative—a critical step towards fostering citizen identification with that institution, and, by extension, towards fostering a national political identity. Furthermore, by overhauling the federal institution of government itself and increasing direct citizen participation in the federal process while decentralizing federal responsibilities, the conditions for intra-governmental harmony and productivity are established and democracy is maximized. Both of these function to promote national unity by maintaining a sociopolitical sensibility that is akin to that of a neighbourhood.

Standard of Living

It is important to recognize that "standard of living" involves (or should involve) more than just material assets and disposable incomes—it should also encompass quality of life; that is to say, that which we might include in a theoretical account of the good life, namely leisure, social and recreational activity, spiritual fulfillment. The value that one derives from being part of a neighbourhood cannot be adequately captured in the size of one's house and quality of one's possessions in relation to those of one's neighbours—it also involves one's relations with those neighbours, with friendships, with participation in neighbourhood activities, and with the amount of time spent lounging in the park or on the porch sipping iced tea.

The above proposal for unity, by increasing the opportunities for individual participation in the political process and by improving relations among different groups, would positively affect our quality of life and therefore contribute to the improvement of the standard of living in Canada. It may also indirectly improve the standard of living by putting federal dollars to use more effectively. While the combined proportionally representative electoral system and Constituency

Association system might appear to be a potentially expensive enterprise, these costs would be minimal once offset by certain structural changes and would represent a more efficient use of funds. The reduction in the number of constituencies and members of Parliament would offset some of the costs of maintaining a system of Constituency Associations, as would the elimination of the Senate. The cost of maintaining an often ineffectual Upper House would be transferred to the maintenance of Constituency Associations—and those funds would be directly channelled into those communities. Furthermore, the decentralization of certain federal jurisdictions would reduce federal costs and reduce the amount of wasted funds on overlapping programs.[6]

Another means of improving the standard of living in Canada—again rooted in the neighbourhood philosophy—would be the promotion of volunteering. For example, a minimum number of volunteer hours might be a requirement, or a condition for additional benefits, for those on social assistance. For others, volunteer activity could be rewarded with tax credits. Increased volunteer activity would serve a number of purposes: it would facilitate skills development and networking for the unemployed, it would immediately provide much-needed resources for many social, cultural, and educational programs, and it would contribute to the development of community spirit. It would also make use of the vast, untapped human resources contained in that portion of our society that is unemployed while avoiding the problem of displacing other (employed) workers.

Mandatory volunteer service could be especially productive in the area of skills training.[7] In a neighbourhood, external "experts" are not hired to baby-sit, give lawn-care advice, or help kids with tough math questions—friends and neighbours are consulted and skills are shared. The same principle can work for the writ-large neighbourhood of Canada: the unemployed office manager might share office skills as a fulfillment of minimal volunteer requirements or to qualify for additional social assistance benefits, the retired computer programmer might spend a few hours a week teaching computer skills, or the small-business owner might donate a couple hours to giving advice to would-be entrepreneurs, in order to qualify for potential tax credits.

What is important here is that social responsibility ultimately becomes the enterprise of all Canadians, and not just of government.

Incentives are clearly necessary to promote social activity (such as volunteer work), but such activity would, one hopes, become an entrenched feature of Canadian life and facilitate the development of a social ethic that emphasizes community, shared responsibility, and public and individual initiative. In the process of building and improving our social, political, and economic neighbourhoods, perhaps we will construct a true, Canadian neighbourhood.

The neighbourhood analogy may not fit the Canadian context perfectly—analogies rarely do—but it is useful as an outline for a new Canadian identity and a shift in public values. Canada, and Canadians, have the raw materials to create a truly great nation; that creation can only occur, however, if we approach the task in the spirit of cooperation and with the common goal of promoting prosperity and harmony. Truly great neighbourhoods and communities utilize all of their available resources, human and otherwise, and respect the independence of their distinct members while promoting and preserving the good of the community. For each of us, our homes, communities, and provinces are our castles—our nation is our shared kingdom.

Notes

1. I use as my model my own experience of neighbourhood, which was, to a large degree, suburban middle class. There were, however, different socioeconomic groups and ethnic groups represented in that neighbourhood, and I suspect that this is true for many neighbourhoods. I acknowledge that there are many varieties of neighbourhood/community, but I believe that the underlying principles are the same.
2. In the current system there exists a wide variety of choice on any given ballot due to the large number of parties that participate. However, the single-member plurality system disproportionately favours the large, established parties and the front-running parties—because of this, votes for minor parties are often "wasted" votes. Real choice, therefore, is extremely limited in single-member plurality systems.
3. Paul Barker, "Voting for Trouble," in *Contemporary Political Issues*, eds. Mark Charlton and Paul Barker, Nelson Canada, Scarborough, 1994, p. 302.

4. I have been influenced, in the development of the constituency-association model, by the work of Professor Vaughn Lyon, who introduced the idea of Canadian community parliaments. See Lyon, "Houses of Citizens," *Policy Options* (volume 5, number 2, 1984), page 43, and "Parties and Democracy: A Critical View," *Canadian Parties in Transition*, eds. A.-G. Gagnon and A.B. Tanguay, (Scarborough: Nelson-Canada, 1995).

5. Legislation would be enacted to require employers to provide those selected with leaves of absence, and those selected would have the option of declining to participate. The brevity of this proposal precludes a detailed outline of the mechanics of this system.

6. The provinces would handle those jurisdictions more efficiently—Canada has a long history of provincial innovation in policies and programs.

7. For government-funded programs, I would emphasize training and support in entrepreneurial endeavours over straight basic training—in other words, encourage those who would set up lemonade stands and do freelance leaf-raking in the Canadian neighbourhood. The core of Canada's unemployment problem is not a surplus of untrained workers, but a lack of jobs—for this reason, excessive spending on training is misguided.

Crafting a New
Canadian Constitution

TODD STRANG

TODD STRANG

A resident of Lawn, Newfoundland, Todd is currently completing his final year of a Bachelor of Arts in Political Science at Memorial University in St. John's. His honours thesis will examine the prospects for Aboriginal self-government in Canada. He received the Governor General's medal for Outstanding Achievement in his final year of high school. Todd intends to enter law school upon graduation. Some of his leisure activities include mountain biking, jogging, and swimming.

If I were Prime Minister of Canada, I would work diligently to improve living standards and unite the country. Through innovative and radical reorganization of the existing federal system and a new approach to economics, the rapid decline of the Canadian state would be stopped and reversed.

Current constitutional arrangements in Canada are the product of the Victorian era. *The Constitution Act, 1982*, is a relic that represents Canada's past connection with Great Britain. The document's principle form has changed little since 1867 when it was the *British North America Act*. For Canadians living in the 20th century, this outdated non-Canadian creation is a source of division between anglophones and francophones, the two largest ethnolinguistic groups in Canada.

If I were Prime Minister, I would move to eliminate the *Constitution Act* as we know it and replace it with a new Canadian creation. It would reflect the diversity of Canadian society as well as the values and morals that are essential to Canadian political culture. The new Constitution would accommodate the needs of each province so no one province would feel that it was being treated in an unequal manner.

The new Constitution would differ with respect to the enumeration of federal and provincial powers as they are spelled out by sections 91 and 92 of the *Constitution Act, 1982*. Instead of two clauses, there would be 10 individual provincial clauses, a federal clause, a territorial clause, and an Aboriginal self-government clause.

Each province would have control over the areas of jurisdiction it deems to be important. Different provinces would not necessarily have control over identical areas of jurisdiction. A province could delegate some of its enumerated powers to the federal government if it was desired, but this in no way would surrender those specific powers.

The clause listing federal powers would be similar to the one that is in place now. However, many of the federal powers that are present now would be in the provincial clauses and not in the federal one. There would be an important qualification, as well. If a new power were to emerge that was not enumerated, it would not immediately fall under federal jurisdiction, as is the case now. If it dealt with Aboriginal or territorial matters it would come under joint federal–provincial control. Upon negotiation with the relevant parties, these powers could be transferred. If the matter was of importance to the provinces, it would fall under exclusive provincial control and if it was exclusively federal, it would fall under federal control. If a dispute arose over to whom jurisdiction and power belonged, the matter would be referred to the Supreme Court for a decision.

As a result of this new form of decentralization and practice of unique asymmetrical federalism, diverse interests and groups in society could be accommodated and satisfied. This would reduce the political hypersensitivity that exists in Canada at present and meet demands for effective political reform. It would reduce regional and linguistic conflicts and help maintain unity in the country.

One part of the current Constitution that would remain intact would be the Charter of Rights and Freedoms. Some sections might be modified and others strengthened but its principle form would remain. The Charter is a Canadian invention that reflects the core values and beliefs of Canadians. It is essential to promoting a better and fairer Canada.

It will be necessary to resolve ongoing disputes with Canada's Aboriginal peoples. As Prime Minister, I would move to allow for the creation of Aboriginal self-government. This is their inherent right, which they never surrendered. It would be another order of government with a defined jurisdiction spelled out in a specific clause in the Constitution. Aboriginal governments would have power in areas of taxation, civil and criminal matters, resource development, and so forth. The Criminal Code and Charter of Rights would still apply to this order of government. Self-government would be limited to reserves and land obtained through land-claim settlements. Non-Aboriginal people in areas under Aboriginal control could choose to be governed by Aboriginal or provincial laws. It is necessary to resolve disputes between the Aboriginal governments and the governments of Canada because the issue is a political tinderbox. Recent history with roadblocks, stand-offs, and armed conflicts reflect this very much.

Aboriginal self-government would be funded a number of different ways. Part of the money would come from federal transfers. This would come from the money now spent by the federal government on reserves and from the budget of the Department of Indian Affairs, which would be abolished upon the creation of such a form of government. Other sources of funding would come from the Aboriginal government's taxation power on its territory, as well as from money obtained from resource development profits on Aboriginal territory.

If I were Prime Minister, the form of Parliament and the electoral system would be changed. The single-member district plurality system over-represents the majority party in the House of Commons and in no way reflects its true percentage of the popular vote. Furthermore, the Senate is an appointed body that is not democratically elected. It is a group of aged elites who are out of touch with mainstream Canadians. This is a contradiction to Canada's democratic nature.

The reformed House of Commons would consist of 350 members. These would be chosen by a different system from the current one. There would be 175 seats chosen by the single-member district plurality method more commonly known as the "first past the post" system. The remaining 175 seats would be chosen by a different method known as proportional representation. This method involves people voting for specific parties that offer slates of candidates. The 175 seats chosen by proportional representation would be used to adjust each party's percentage of seats in the House of Commons so it would reflect that party's actual percentage of the popular vote. This would almost entirely eliminate the chance of a majority government. Parties would be forced to cooperate to arrive at decisions and policies. This would reduce the influence of elites and partisan practices in Canadian politics. It would mean more groups in society would have influence and input into the political process and this would serve as a uniting force.

The Senate would also be modified. It would become an elected body. The new, revised Senate would consist of 70 members. Each province would elect six senators, each territory would elect two, and the Aboriginal governments across Canada would elect six senators by a nationwide referendum that would offer slates of Aboriginal candidates. All legislation would have to pass in equal form in the House of Commons and the Senate. The reform of the Senate would further reduce elite control. It would give regional representatives input into the policy-making process and enhance the democratic nature of the Canadian state.

As Prime Minister, I would introduce term limits on the careers of politicians. Members of Parliament would be limited to three terms of five years, to a maximum of 15 years. Senators would be elected once every six years and would be limited to two terms to a maximum of 12 years. The Prime Minister would be eligible to serve as Prime Minister for two terms up to a maximum of 10 years. The Prime Minister's career could extend beyond the normal three terms for ordinary members of Parliament but not beyond four terms. The limit on the Prime Minister's overall career, including time as an ordinary member of Parliament and later as Prime Minister, would be 20 years. This would reduce the number of older, long-serving politicians and make room for young, talented individuals. It would reduce the power of elite interests to whom many older politicians feel indebted for aiding their political careers.

As Prime Minister, I would eliminate the monarchy's role in Canadian politics. The Prime Minister would become the head of state and the head of government. The Queen and the Governor General would no longer be recognized. This would help develop a more pure Canadian political culture and environment. This is a long-needed move, because the monarchy has little relevance to modern Canadian society. The monarchy has no meaning to French Canadians nor to many Canadians who come from a non-British background. Even for a majority of English Canadians of British descent, the monarchy is a remnant of the past with no place in Canada today.

As Prime Minister, I would work to improve the economy and living standards of Canadians. Past economic practices have negatively impacted the economy. Persistently run deficits and accumulated debt over one-half trillion dollars are restricting the discretionary spending power of the federal and provincial governments. Astronomical levels of personal income tax have repeatedly led to the contraction of disposable income of average Canadians and have inevitably led to a reduced standard of living for many workers in the country today. As Prime Minister, I would change the nature of the tax system in Canada today. I would strive to make the tax system more efficient, more cost effective, and more friendly to lower income Canadians.

The present system of personal income tax would be eliminated. This would be replaced with a flat tax that would be fixed at a certain percentage. This tax would eliminate the need for complicated tax returns and would reduce time, effort, and cost for working Canadians. It would also mean less bureaucracy, which in turn would save all Canadian tax payers money. This tax would only apply to individuals or families whose income was more than $40,000. Families whose income is less than $40,000 would be exempt from the tax. This would give them more money to meet their personal needs adequately.

Corporate income taxes would be affected as well. As Prime Minister, I would seek to collect the billions of dollars in outstanding corporate income taxes and move to create harsh penalties for corporations that use sophisticated, illegal tax-avoidance schemes. I would also raise corporate income taxes by five percent. This would be refundable if the corporation spent the total amount of that five percent in research and development or expansion in Canada. This would help strengthen the basis of the Canadian economy for the future.

As Prime Minister, I would strive to get a national sales tax, which would be integrated into the price of products. This would reduce the massive bureaucracy that is present with the Goods and Services Tax. The reduction in bureaucracy and red tape would save government, business, and consumers money.

My government would introduce a new technology tax. This would be a three-percent tax that would be built into the price of such technological commodities as computers, programs, CDs, cellular phones, and so on. It would be similar to a gasoline tax. Proceeds from this tax would be funnelled into a special fund. Money in this fund would be given to various colleges and universities in the form of grants to further innovative research in new technologies for the future. This would help alleviate the funding cuts that have taken place in post-secondary education and help to develop Canadian technological expertise for the future.

As Prime Minister, I would change the Constitution with respect to economic matters. Budgets would have to be balanced unless three quarters of the legislature approved of a deficit. Even in this case, a deficit could only grow at the same percentage as gross domestic product. Only in times of war or extreme crisis could unlimited deficits be run. This would bring fiscal responsibility to government and protect future young Canadians from inheriting a debt any larger than the one we have inherited today.

There would also be a social clause placed in the Constitution. This would define healthcare and education transfers to the provinces from the federal government. There would be minimum percentages of transfers set and recognized for each province that would take into account population and economic output. This would guarantee a measure of stability to health care and education in Canada today.

As Prime Minister, I would seek to expand trade further. I would encourage trade missions of business and government representatives to other countries. I would seek to further free trade with more nations. This would be contingent upon their economies being strong, their currencies stable, and their ratio of debt to gross domestic product acceptable. I would press harder for closer trade relations with Japan and other countries in the Asia-Pacific area. I would also press for closer economic relations with the European Union. These areas have the strongest economies in the world and Canada has not tapped this area to its fullest potential.

Canada today faces many challenges. The very future of the country is at stake. Not only is there a threat to national unity but economic stability and prosperity are also at stake. Past and current attempts by politicians have not worked and will not work. Therefore, as Prime Minister, I would take a new approach to politics and economics. A massive reorganization or the structure and instruments of government would take place. As a result of new economic practices and a new organization of government, the rapid decline of the Canadian state would be stopped and unity and prosperity will begin and ensure all Canadians will have a bright future.

A New Strength for Canadians

WALTER DANIEL PARSONS

WALTER DANIEL PARSONS

A resident of Spaniard's Bay, Newfoundland, Walter Parsons is entering the third year of the Bachelor of Science in Engineering program at the University of New Brunswick in Fredericton. In 1994, he received a Canada Scholarship for Science and Engineering and in 1995 was the recipient of the John H. Fulton Memorial Scholarship in Electrical Engineering. He is actively involved in youth parliament, both in Newfoundland and in Nova Scotia, and in 1994 was elected leader of the opposition at the Newfoundland and Labrador provincial session. That same year, he earned third place in a provincial public-speaking competition. Walter enjoys basketball, table tennis, croquet, and mountain biking and is an active amateur astronomer. He intends to pursue a career in biomedical engineering.

As Canadians we have always shared a deep pride in our country despite our many distinct cultural needs. Our compromising attitudes have held us together in a remarkably successful union. Recently, however, adverse socioeconomic conditions have thrust our federation into disrepair. Canada has fallen victim to the pressures of high unemployment, declining living standards, and regional demands for power and special recognition. Alarmingly, many Canadians predict that our country will be severed by its division along cultural and linguistic boundaries. I refuse to accept this dismal prognosis, as it is entirely uncharacteristic of our Canadian identity. I believe that we can restructure our federation to accommodate all Canadians. Perhaps fundamental change in the way we govern our country can restore the unity and prosperity required for long-term national stability.

If I were Prime Minister of Canada, I would aim to run our government as a nationwide forum for constructive contributions, using all possible avenues to gather the ideas and concerns of citizens. Such an endeavour would be reflected in my own efforts to listen to the concerns of people in all geographic regions of Canada. Twice a month, I would visit a different federal constituency. Along with the local member of Parliament, I would take time to speak with Canadians who are concerned with our future. I would make personal efforts to congratulate successful Canadians. These people, as well as those who have been less successful, would be asked to discuss our nation's problems and brainstorm possible solutions. I would invite all Canadians, from stockbrokers in Vancouver to iron ore miners in Labrador City, to replace the traditional bureaucratic policy consultants and play an active role in the development of my policies.

Government institutions would also be redesigned to speak better for all Canadians. Specifically, changes would be implemented to strengthen responsible democracy in Parliament. I would have an obligation to oppose any government assembly that did not effectively reflect the realities of our people. Consequently, I would overhaul the existing Senate and endorse the resurrection of the Upper House as a new legislative body with a vastly different role and composition.

Each province would be entitled to six senators in the new chamber. Allowing for equal representation of provinces in the Senate would be aimed at counteracting the central Canadian domination of the House of Commons. Changes in the way senators are appointed would also further my efforts to increase democracy in Canada's government. Senators would be selected randomly from the voters' list of each province, in much the same way juries are chosen. Upon appointment, each would be subject to a Supreme Court veto before taking office. The senatorial selection process would ensure that Canadians from various professions and diverse interests would be represented in government, giving the legislators of our country real input from those who know Canada best. The Senate would become a "House of the Common Man," and would draw strength from its apolitical composition. Farmers, miners, and fishermen would have representation equal to that of lawyers, business people, and politicians.

Members of the Upper House would serve only one term, equal to the life of one government in the House of Commons. The Senate would no longer initiate legislation, but all Commons bills would be subject to Senate approval. Joint Commons–Senate committees would work to reconcile any differences the two chambers may have. If the two houses could not reach a compromise after a six-month interval, a joint sitting of the Senate and the House of Commons would decide, by a simple majority, which bills are to become law. In such a joint sitting, the size of the House of Commons relative to the Senate would give the Commons clear legislative authority. Consequently, the House of Commons would retain its position as the primary legislative body, and the Senate would serve as a complementary second chamber designed to be sensitive to regional and local concerns.

My government would also work toward reforming the House of Commons. As Prime Minister, I would insist on free votes on most government legislation. I would demand solidarity only on central matters such as the budget and the Speech from the Throne. My colleagues, and those in the opposition parties, would be encouraged to visit their constituencies regularly to collect input on all matters raised in Parliament. This input would be carried directly into the federation's decision-making processes.

Establishing a fixed number of seats for the Commons would also be a priority. Under the current scheme, the number of Commons seats is increased during each reallocation. I would introduce legislation to set the number of sitting members at 301, and allow for a redistribution of existing seats every 10 years. Population would determine the number of seats per province, but each would be guaranteed a minimum of four. In addition, the territories would each be allocated two seats.

Undeniably, these changes to our Parliament would be a necessary first step toward improving the accessibility of the Canadian government. Renewal of the structure of the Canadian federation would also be undertaken, with significant attention directed towards better accommodating the distinct mix of cultures that makes up our country.

On October 30, 1995, the people of Quebec voted 51 percent to 49 percent to remain in Canada. Less than five months later, a CBC poll suggested that, if another referendum were held, 51 percent of voters would opt for sovereignty. More encouraging, however, is that the same poll found that nearly two thirds of Quebeckers would choose a renewed Canadian federation over an independent Quebec. There is clearly something to be learned from these results. The people of Quebec are not content with the present Canadian framework. We have known this for a long time. They have revitalized their call for a renewed, more flexible union. Canada must be made more sympathetic to regional concerns, especially to those inside Quebec. As Prime Minister, the construction of a more workable federation would be the focus of my mandate.

Before taking any approaches to restructuring Canada, all concerns about the possibility of another Quebec referendum must be put to rest. The existence of this possibility is nothing more than an obstacle to all productive negotiations. As Prime Minister, I would use my constitutional power of disallowance to ensure that no referendum on sovereignty would be held without the approval of the federal government. If a federally sanctioned referendum were held, it would involve a fair and simple question asking the people of Quebec to decide between Canada and complete independence. In addition, I would resolve that any vote to create an independent Quebec would be followed by referendums in every constituency, allowing residents to decide between joining the new nation and remaining in Canada.

Once having obstructed the threat of separation, my government would work to ensure that the people of Quebec would have the opportunity to work collectively with other Canadians to develop a new blueprint for Canada. I would propose a realignment of government jurisdictions to ensure government powers are exercised where they best serve the Canadian people. Provincial governments would be given significant opportunities to take control of selected shared-cost programs. Federal control over these programs would be delegated and replaced by the enforcement of federal standards. I would argue that symmetry and equality can be maintained while allowing provinces to take control of their own affairs to different degrees.

I would employ a provision, found in section 94 of the Constitution, which presents an alternative approach to federal symmetry. In any decision regarding the reduction of federal government authority, all provinces would be considered equally and would receive equal offers of powers. If Quebec, or any other province, demands a set of 10 new powers, the 10 powers could be given to all the provinces. Those provinces opposed to decentralization could pass some or all of these powers back to the federal government, thus opting in to federal jurisdiction. I would also allow provinces to opt out of federal jurisdiction, provided any province interested could guarantee adherence to federal standards and provide equitable services with existing funds.

Under my leadership, the Canadian federation would always be open to new ideas and new alliances. In particular, I would actively seek out new partnerships with the many British dependencies in North America. These nations, the majority of which are semi-independent colonies of Great Britain, would be invited to participate in free-trade negotiations and other forms of economic cooperation with Canada. I would explore the possibility of expanding Canada's economic union to include those political units in North America that share our vision for a healthy social and economic environment. This integration could eventually lead to an expanded federation, through offers of monetary and perhaps political union. Such an expansion would highlight the rewards of a federation of autonomous provinces, and would offer small dependencies both the political liberty of self-determination and the economic stability of federalism.

As Prime Minister I would make substantial efforts to recognize the Aboriginal peoples of Canada. I would eliminate the Department of Indian Affairs and endorse Native self-government. Before its implementation, self-government would be thoroughly defined and its structure firmly established through multilateral negotiations with all

Aboriginal nations and all 10 provinces. Specifically, I would back the creation of a new province, to be composed of all the Aboriginal communities and reserves across the country. This new province would be physically discontinuous, linked by a variety of accessible communications technologies. The Aboriginal budget would be handed over to the newly formed provincial government, after a phase-in period of at least 10 years. During this time, I would establish a forum to gather ideas on the most effective means of investing the funds in the creation of sustainable industry and employment.

The new province could be run as a federation within a federation, to ensure representation from all Aboriginal nations in Canada. It would also ensure that non-status Aboriginals and those living outside Aboriginal communities would be represented in the new political entity. This plan would guarantee adequate First Nations representation in the House of Commons, the Senate, First Ministers conferences, and all future constitutional negotiations, without further necessitating the application of quotas or other "reverse discrimination" in government. Today, with the impending possibility of Quebec separation, the reasons for the creation of this new province are even more obvious. It may be the only way to ensure that Canada's First Nations retain their right to self-determination in the event of a unilateral declaration of independence by Quebec.

Another key aspect of my mandate would be the restructuring of the present social assistance programs. My government would redefine these programs to maintain sufficient income protection for the poor in our society, while reducing waste, discouraging abuse, reducing government dependency, and promoting self-reliance. This redefinition of our social safety net would include significant measures to support work initiatives. I would replace the entire patchwork of existing income maintenance programs (employment insurance, the Canada Pension Plan, seniors' benefits, and provincial welfare programs) with a "negative income tax." This scheme would include the establishment of a guaranteed annual income for all Canadian citizens. The federal government would provide income subsidies for persons whose personal income falls below a certain level.

Under the plan, every Canadian citizen would be guaranteed an annual income of $10,000. For every dollar a person earns, 50 cents in benefits would be reclaimed. Consequently, a person earning $10,000 would receive $5,000 in government benefits, for a total income of $15,000. A person earning $20,000 or more would receive no government benefits.

Canadians would be encouraged to take complete control over planning for their own retirement. The current Canada and Quebec pension plans lead to further reliance on government and effectively force people to pay into a pension plan over which they have no control. Although the guaranteed annual income would provide sufficient protection against poverty, it would certainly not ensure a lavish lifestyle. My plan would encourage workers to invest in RRSPs and other long-term investments, and would allow them to decide the specifics of their own retirement plans.

The key to success in this new approach would be the strategic investment of the conserved funds. Funds saved through the implementation of this program would be invested in the creation of employment in diverse sectors of the economy. My government would promote the Canadian Forces as a viable means of securing a successful career, and would invest in increasing the number of annual recruits and the number of available employment opportunities. Various forms of community service work and environmental preservation projects would also be developed with the new funds. Canadians would be encouraged to work in different regions of Canada, to gain an understanding and an appreciation of our extensive cultural diversity.

The government of this country must begin to understand the realities of Canada. We are a mosaic of distinct peoples, with a variety of languages and cultures. Despite these differences, we share certain aspirations. Canadians work for economic prosperity and good relations with each other and with the rest of the world. For more than a century, Canada has stood for peace, democracy, compromise, equality, and prevention of poverty. These ideals can be preserved well into the future, if the necessary first steps are taken today. I have suggested that certain reforms to our government and to our social programs will be necessary. These changes, once in place, will contribute largely to the unity and prosperity of our homeland and will ensure that Canada remains the envy of the global community.

A Six-Point Strategic Plan to Build on Our Economic, Political, and Social Strengths

KARL VILLENEUVE

KARL VILLENEUVE

Karl is entering the final year of study in a Bachelor in Business Administration at Bishop's University in Lennoxville, Quebec. A native of Montreal, Karl plays defensive back for the Bishop's Gaitors football team. In high school, he was spokesman for Les Ambassadeurs de paix, a select group of Quebec teenagers sent to take messages of peace to students in the former USSR. A green belt in karate and a member of Ducks Unlimited, Karl enjoys duck painting and collecting fishing reels. His career ambition is to own and operate his own business.

The main economic goal of a government is to help its citizens by establishing a high and increasing standard of living. Historically, we can say that Canada has succeeded. Yet, today economic reality indicates to us that Canada is at an economic turning point. Every day we see signs that Canadian industry has difficulties adapting to a new competitive environment. Workers are laid off and companies are closing or restructuring. On the political side, the country is in a continuing crisis. Quebec's future in Confederation is uncertain and this fact adds uncertainty to an already shaky economy. If this trend continues, our standard of living will deteriorate. Canadians and the Canadian government must face this reality and take corrective action. The situation is urgent and calls for effective solutions if we do not want future generations to pay for our mistakes.

The foundation of a country's economy is productivity. Canada is in a crisis because the growth of its productivity has not kept stride with the other industrialized countries. Productivity is very important because it influences the wealth and the well-being of the entire population, as well as of individual companies. To achieve lasting productivity, an economy must always develop and improve itself.

There is a basis for productivity already in place in Canada that should help firms and industries in their battle for international competitiveness. Canadian industry profits from a good infrastructure, a number of universities and other research facilities, and educated human resources with proven capabilities. The challenge is to redefine government policies and industry strategies that grow and build on these strengths in order to improve living standards and unite the country.

Ingredients of an Economic Dream

As Prime Minister of Canada, I would come up with a new vision for the Canadian economy. A vision in which Canada's plentiful natural resources are fully used. A vision in which companies and governments concentrate on developing advanced skills and technology. A vision in which Canadian firms compete globally. A vision in which Canada is a united country. To realize this vision, I would help Canadian businesses compete differently. I would assist them in their transition into more complex segments of industry. I would then develop many precise steps to maximize productivity and improve the dynamism of the economy. These steps would be part of a grand strategy.

The Grand Economic Objectives

- *Develop an innovative economy.* Innovation is the key to economic modernization and increased prosperity. Canadian companies must stress innovation in order to develop competitive advantages. Governments must adjust their policies in order to support this objective.
- *Expand more complex segments of the natural resources industry.* Natural resources are responsible for a major part of Canada's wealth. However, the high concentration of exports of non-processed resources means that Canada has failed to upgrade its competitive advantage in terms of production, marketing, and related technology. This leaves Canada very weak in the face of shifting commodity prices, substituted technologies, and competitors that offer lower costs.
- *Eliminate barriers to productivity.* This must be a priority for firms and governments. Governments should encourage a greater concentration on work, investment, and skill development.
- *Construct a Canada based on regional strengths.* Numerous government policies in Canada have aimed at economic diversification rather than at competitive advantage, a strategy that needs to be changed. We need a strategy that concentrates on building industry groups according to proven strengths.
- *Achieve total free trade inside Canada.* Canada must become a true single market. Competitiveness in a number of industries has been slowed by internal barriers to trade, investment, and labour mobility. It is urgent that the federal government come up with new proposals for constitutional reform in order to accelerate the transition towards internal free trade and a strengthened Canadian union. A more liberal economy should help to unite Canada.

- *Encourage foreign firms to establish home bases in Canada.* Foreign companies that exist in Canada only to serve the Canadian market will leave if their productivity doesn't equal their operations elsewhere. Therefore, Canadian policies must contribute by encouraging innovation and productivity.
- *Create a stable microeconomic environment.* Monetary, fiscal, tax, and regulatory policies should aim at lowering inflation, balancing public expenses, and creating a stable economic climate. This will consequently lower capital costs and help stimulate investments.

In light of these points, it is fair to assume that government policy should aim at building the skills, research infrastructure, and other boosts that industry needs. Using legislation, competitive policy, and policy in other areas, my government would create an economic environment that facilitates improved and growing productivity.

The Role of the Government

Canadian government policies should be developed so as to assist Canadian industries achieve international competitive success. To that end, my government would take different actions:
- *Minimize direct intervention by government.* Direct governmental intervention often leads to unhealthy dependence on government by industry. It often permits the survival of non-competitive firms. Federal and provincial governments should use indirect intervention to encourage competitiveness. Indirect intervention is more efficient at improving infrastructures and developing human resources as well as creating economic policies that promote invest ment and upgrading.
- *Use incentives instead of grants.* Grants offered to selected firms rarely translate into real competitive advantages. It is highly improbable that governments can adequately choose "winners." It is not government's job anyway. Incentives that encourage firms to upgrade skills or improve infrastructure are more effective policy tools.
- *Revise social policies.* Competitiveness and social goals tend to be linked in the long run. Competitive industries lead to a stronger national economy, which in turn can meet social goals. It is very

important that social goals do not hinder economic development or productivity. A competitive advantage will help achieve social goals, and not the reverse.

- *Improve coordination of intergovernmental policies.* The burden imposed by the Canadian government on the economy is very heavy. It is magnified by all the counter-productive interactions between the federal and provincial governments. Canadians pay a high price for maintaining such an ineffective bureaucracy at both levels and do not receive their money's worth. The federal government must improve the collaboration and coordination between Ottawa and the provinces.

- *Support and encourage foreign investment.* Foreign investment is essential to the Canadian economy. Foreign firms are often more efficiently run and more technologically advanced than domestic firms. An important objective of my government's economic policy would be to improve the Canadian economic environment so those firms are not limited to sourcing raw materials but can broaden the nature of their economic operations over time.

- *Develop a stable macroeconomic environment.* The major objective for the Canadian government is to reduce its deficit. Doing so will enable it to pursue other goals that will support competitiveness, such as lowering inflation, increasing the national savings rate, and balancing public-sector spending. Large deficits are the most critical problem facing Canada today. Therefore, reducing government deficits is imperative if Canada wants to compete in the future.

Implications for the Government

When a government decides that improving productivity is important, there are three areas to consider: technological productivity, worker productivity, and specific policies.

There are significant weaknesses in the areas of technological development and acceptance. Encouraging the private sector to do more research and development and to switch to new technologies should be a priority for the government. Government must develop clear policies that encourage firms to consider, for example, jointly funding and participating in research conducted at university centres. Therefore, my government would:

- *Create strong links between universities, government laboratories, and industry.* Government must emphasize synergy and links between these sectors in order to achieve a greater rate of technological development.

- *Encourage specialization among universities.* More specialization is needed to achieve competitive advantage. Universities should understand that being all things to all people is a recipe for mediocrity. Such specialization has been discouraged by current funding mechanisms.

Increasing worker productivity is a big challenge for Canada. Improved human resources are necessary if we want Canadian firms to be more competitive. In order to respond to new challenges offered by the economy, my government would take new initiatives in a number of areas:

- *Provide more training for the unemployed.* The government, in conjunction with industry, must develop efficient training programs that will truly respond to the needs of employers.

- *Encourage training in the private sector.* Government should take measures to stimulate more training. Government could give tax exemptions or credits to encourage training.

- *Establish high educational standards.* Canada is almost the only one among advanced countries that does not have national educational standards. In other countries, such standards are a prime factor in encouraging high achievement.

- *Put more emphasis on developing practical abilities and science skills.* Canada does not have enough engineers, scientists, and technical workers in its workforce. School curriculums should be remodelled so that they stress the importance of science, mathematics, and other technical disciplines.

- *Expand apprenticeship programs.* It is urgent that Canada upgrade its apprenticeship training in order to develop a pool of highly skilled workers.

- *Direct university funding to support competitiveness.* Funds should be geared towards universities that have programs directly linked to competitiveness. The privatization of certain programs or universities should be considered.

Canadian government policies for regional and industrial development have often worked against the goal of building strong, geographically concentrated groups of industry. My government policies would be developed to meet new needs as follows:

- *Make sure that all government policies aim at developing strong industrial groups.*
- *Create policies that develop regional strengths.* A region often has a competitive advantage; government should help to strengthen it.
- *Let regions specialize by investing in regional infrastructures related to the needs of specific industries.*

Policy Strategies

Government can improve the competitiveness by encouraging a stable economic environment that favours investments and skill upgrading and by assuring healthy competition. Therefore, to stimulate the competitive advantage, my government would apply the following strategies:

- *Rethink the "safety net."* Programs must be directed towards the right people. Ensure that clear incentives are given to unemployed workers to improve their skills.
- *Encourage a stronger relationship between performance and compensation.* Providing employees with the opportunity to invest in the company they work for would be a very efficient way to increase competitiveness. Employees should share the good and the bad times that a company experiences.
- *Develop tax strategies that encourage long-term investment.* To increase its international competitiveness, Canada must invest in training, technology, machinery, and equipment. The results from such investments are often only appreciable over the long term. Therefore, Canada should take measures to increase incentives in long-term investments.
- *Finally, government must move very aggressively to bring back a favourable macroeconomic environment.* The stepping stone to achieving this objective remains the reduction of the deficit.

All these economic actions and policies will succeed only if Canadians can move forward in its attitude. Individuals must accept the new economic reality and understand the foundations of their past prosperity. But instead of looking at the past, Canadians must redefine themselves.

This is why I believe that all these measures must be accompanied by a sound marketing campaign aimed at uniting the country. The ordinary Canadian thinks that this country has serious economic and political problems. This is true, but why not look at all the positive advantages of being Canadian? This country offers incredible advantages to its citizens. Our society is civilized; our judicial system is fair; we have a moral contract among citizens; we have equality in employment; we have freedom of choice and expression so we can live and raise our children in a tolerant climate, protected from extreme racist or religious conflicts.

All immigrants who come to Canada are amazed by the quality of life here. When they compare our standard of living to the country they are from, they know we are fortunate. In their respective countries, only the elite can take vacations during the winter; only the elite can possess a membership in a golf club or have access to a ski hill. Those immigrants are also amazed by the Canadian nature, which is so present and so accessible.

Therefore, my government would play up Canada's reputation. The great spaces, the mountains, the wilderness, the wild forests. My government would develop a true Canadian identity. An identity that projects a positive image and that includes every Canadian. An identity that takes into account cultural differences. For example, my strategy would project a specific image of each region but find general links among all of them.

As the Prime Minister of Canada, I would remind Canadians of the luck they have of living in such a wonderful country. Our country does not make war; we chose peace a long time ago. Peace is a constitutional principle equal to the principles of order and responsible government. Canadians who travel soon realize that their nationality opens many doors. The reason why we benefit from such a reputation is simple but extraordinary: we owe it to our fathers who bravely fought to defend justice on all continents. In the worst hours of World War I, Canadians were said to be the best soldiers.

During World War II, our army was the principal ally of Great Britain, which was completely isolated before Hitler's army.

Since the end of those hostilities, Canadians have always tried to maintain peace throughout the world. Our soldiers can function in the two official languages and are problem-solvers and masters of negotiation. As Prime Minister, I would also stress that our country must take advantage of having two great cultures living together. This could be a tremendous strength if we could put our differences aside and develop a relationship based on respect, equality, and mutual understanding.

Canada is at a crossroads. Government action must be wiser than ever. The decisions that will be taken in the next few years will determine our future. Let's understand the urgent need to develop excellent strategic policies in order to continue to enjoy one of the greatest standards of living in the world.

Notes

1. Porter, Michael E., *Canada at the Crossroads*, Harvard Business School, October 1991.
2. Daft, Richard L., *Management*, Holt, Rinehart and Winston of Canada, 1992.
3. Bulletin de la Banque Royale, vol. 77, n.2, Printemps 1996.

PART TWO

"And if *we* were Prime Minister…"

To Act As a Canadian: Now We've Got to "Win The Peace"

GRAEME DECARIE

GRAEME DECARIE

Born in Montreal, Graeme Decarie is an associate professor of history at Concordia University. He has a Bachelor of Arts from Sir George Williams University in Montreal, a Master of Arts from Acadia University, and a doctorate from Queen's University. He taught at the University of Prince Edward Island before joining Concordia and also worked as an elementary and high school teacher. He has served for many years on the provincial executive of Alliance Quebec, was an editorialist for CBC Radio and columnist for the Montreal *Gazette* and several other publications. For the past three years, Dr. Decarie has been a daily editorialist on CJAD Radio in Montreal.

As the Second World War, with all of its posters and slogans on the home front, came to a close, Canadians paid little attention to a new poster that appeared. But that new poster carried the most important of all the wartime slogans. "We've won the war," it said. "We've won the war. Now we've got to win the peace."

Most were probably too slogan-weary to grasp the meaning of that poster. In any case, it seemed for decades that we had won the peace. For decades, we built a powerful sense of unity and pride based on accomplishments made together and made to benefit all of us— industrial expansion, magnificent engineering achievements such as the St. Lawrence Seaway, a network of social legislation that most of the world could only envy, an education system that at its peak involved fully one quarter of the Canadian population, the beginnings of protecting our environment and ourselves from the plagues of industrialization.

Then, silently, slowly, the achievements withered and, with them, the sense of national unity. Today, we are losing the peace, losing all that so many had suffered and died for to make possible.

It's not hard to see why we're losing. Most of what we can do for each other we do through our governments, federal and provincial. But our governments, like governments all over the world, are losing the power to express our will in legislation. That's why, whatever the differences among their expressed philosophies or programs, most parties act remarkably alike once in power. It isn't because politicians lie about their beliefs (although that can happen, too); it's because they have no power to carry them out. The conventional explanation given for this is that governments can no longer afford to express our will, and there is some truth in that. But the fuller truth is more complex.

The development of what we vaguely call the "global economy" and of free trade has provided wonderful opportunities for economic growth. But it has also given commercial and industrial giants the freedom to ignore the wishes of governments—which means they can afford to ignore our wishes. National and provincial priorities, our priorities, can no longer be enforced as they were even 20 years ago. It is difficult, for example, to demand environmental standards of factories when they can simply move to a country that imposes no standards at all while still selling products on the Canadian market.

To add to the problem, Canada has a constitution designed for the world of 1867, one designed, as it had to be, for a social and economic world that ceased to exist almost a century ago. We live in a world of super-cities and jet transport with a constitution designed for a nation of small towns connected and powered by steam engines. This observation is not, of course, an original one. Over the years it has given rise to armies of pundits with answers. And that is where the problem lies.

The best thing we can do for Canada and for each other is to do what the founders of this country did in the 1860s: don't thrash about blindly for answers but ask questions first, set objectives, and then propose answers.

The founders of Canada were neither philosophers nor idealists. Rather, they were blessed with the typically Canadian traits of the hard-headed, practical problem-solver. Curiously, Canadians seldom think of themselves as a practical people. When they try to define themselves at all, it is usually in jokes: a Canadian is someone who can make love in a canoe; a Canadian is a freeze-dried American. But any serious reading of this country's past shows that practical problem-solving and organization have been dominant characteristics of Canadians throughout their history, ones that have revealed themselves in every area of life.

That passion for organization helps to explain why Canadians are perhaps the only people to have created or organized at least four modern sports—ice hockey, modern lacrosse, North American football, and basketball. It may also explain why the amateur soldiers that Canada sent to France in 1914 became, within two years, a better army than those of the European professionals, who proved unable to adjust to the new conditions of warfare.

In the same way, the practical problems of railway building were meat and drink to Canadians. In just over 30 years, this tiny country (as it was in the 19th century) not only covered itself with more railways per capita than any other country in the world, but also built more of them in Africa, China, and Latin America.

It was these practical, organizing people who faced seemingly impossible problems in 1867. With a home market too small for their developing industries, they had little hope of finding markets outside, particularly in the more industrially advanced Britain and in the

United States where industries were sheltered behind high tariffs. Western expansion and immigration might solve the problem by creating a home market, but that was an enormous challenge for a scattering of tiny colonies that, in any case, couldn't afford the railways that would be needed to supply such a market.

We know, from our history books, that they found their answer in uniting the tiny, scattered colonies into one nation. But they didn't start with the answer. As a practical people, they started with questions. What would the world be like over the next 50 years? What would the major social and economic problems be? Which of those problems were best handled by a central government, and which by provincial governments? Then, and only then, did they design a constitution that was to carry Canada to a future– and it was a constitution that worked very well for the future that was foreseeable in 1867, carrying this country from colonial insignificance to being a major producer for world markets, a railway builder to the world, and a force on the world stage.

Quite unlike the Americans, Canadians did not found their country on a constitution of philosophical principles. A consequence for Americans, incidentally, has been a society so bound by those principles of more than two centuries ago that it has had great difficulty adapting to the social challenges of this century. Canadians chose a different way. Our constitution of 1867 was one of practical, businesslike arrangements. It was not a statement of principle for the ages; it was a plan of development for the near to middle future. Now, what that constitution was designed to do has long since been done. The West has been added to the nation, communications systems link us together, and the commercial and industrial infrastructures have matured.

But now, just as in 1867, we face a world that has changed so rapidly that our means of organizing for it has fallen behind. And, as it falls behind, our institutions become outmoded and wither; we are losing our sense of where we are going together, and, as we lose that, we lose our sense of being Canadians together. What is the single, most important thing we can do to change that?

The single, most important thing we can do is remember the fundamental trait that made this a great country. We can turn our backs on all the power-brokers and idealogues with their narrow and self-serving answers. The Canadian way is not to waste time on the sterile ideologies of centralization versus decentralization or of liberalism versus conservatism versus neoconservatism (whatever those delightfully vague terms might mean). The Canadian way is to define the problem, then to work out practical answers.

As an eminently practical people, we should first ask questions. What are the forces that will affect us over the next 50 years? What must we change to meet those forces? What must we preserve? What do we want this country to be? Change will most certainly come. Either we are not a nation—and we allow the changes simply to happen and suffer accordingly—or we remain a nation by acting as we did in 1867, by taking control of our future.

It is beyond the scope of this essay (indeed it would be contradictory) to lay out the questions and the answers. What follows, then, is not a blueprint for discussion but simply an indication—a very superficial one—of the direction such a discussion might take.

Economically, the next 50 to 100 years are likely to see a continuation and even a broadening of free trade blocs with, incidentally, a strong danger of war among those blocs. High productivity is likely to continue and be combined, as it has throughout most of our history (except in wartime), with high levels of unemployment and underemployment. As productivity and population increase, pressure on the environment could well threaten disaster. Despite the ease of electronic communication, populations will still drift to the cities with an even higher proportion of Canadians living in cities and an increase in the challenges created by urban living.

What Canadians will want, almost certainly, is access to adequate income and services, and it is no platitude to say they must have them. The alternative, to be merely calculating about it, would be severe social unrest probably coupled with manifestations of racism and facism. To continue in a practical vein, a failure to provide for adequate incomes would also destroy commerce.

With those concerns in mind, Canadians might reflect that quarrelling over provincial and federal powers makes as much sense as quarrelling over colonial and village powers would have made in 1867. If the economy is international, with all that means in terms of environmental controls, social legislation, and economic planning, and if any government is to have any influence, then there must be a level of government beyond Ottawa. The international integration of business and, to a considerable degree, the integration of the military have already occurred. Unless we have an integration of government to correspond to other examples of integration that have already happenned, then no government can be meaningful.

There should also be consideration for the constitutional powers of cities. Cities are not only the dynamic centres of society but also are quite different in their needs from the towns and countrysides of the provinces. Yet, under our constitution, cities have no powers of their own and are treated simply as juveniles under the guardianship of provincial governments. For the consequences of that, one need only look at the sad decline of Montreal.

However, none of this is to be taken as a formula, only as an indication of the direction a practical discussion might take. It will certainly be taken as extraordinarily challenging and ambitious, even over-ambitious. For those who consider it too ambitious, consider the alternative of sitting back helplessly while the world rolls over us. For those who consider it too challenging, consider those insignificant colonial leaders of 1867 who had the courage to reach out across a continent.

But the important thing is to start with questions. Having asked the questions, then and only then can we again exploit our historic talent for finding practical solutions. The Canadian way has been not to fight over which level of government gets which power, but to decide what has to be done and then to decide who can most effectively do it. Understanding that and building on our traditional strength is the way to maintain our unity and do things together for each other. Then, at last, we can win the peace.

An Anishinabe Prime Minister

PHIL FONTAINE

PHIL FONTAINE

Larry Philip Fontaine was first elected Grand Chief, Assembly of Manitoba Chiefs, in 1991. He was returned by Acclamation in 1991 and re-elected in 1994. Prior to his election as Grand Chief, Mr. Fontaine served the Assembly of First Nations as Vice-Chief for Manitoba. Until his election, he was Regional Director in the Yukon for the Department of Indian Affairs and Deputy Federal Coordinator of the Native Economic Development Program. In 1981, Mr. Fontaine graduated from the University of Manitoba with a B.A. in Political Studies. He started school speaking only Ojibway and attended residential schools in Fort Alexander and Winnipeg. Today, Mr. Fontaine lives in Winnipeg and has two children, Mike and Maya.

If I were Prime Minister, I would be the first Anishinabe to lead the Government of Canada. Anishinabe is the Ojibway word for ourselves, our people. To be Anishinabe is to be part of a community and culture with a distinctive language, traditions, values, and history. To be Anishinabe is also to share a common history, the history of being Canadian, and contributing to the development to Canada from the outset. But in this history we have also seen imbalances and unfairness in the placement of Anishinabe in Canada. As Prime Minister, I would want to build further on our contributions, address historical injustices, and serve the interests of all Canadians.

As Canadians know, in many respects Canada is the envy of the world. It is seen as one of the best places in the world to live, with a very high standard of living. The world is aware that, as Canadians, we have the freedom to create and fulfill opportunities, and that basic necessities such as health care, education, and potable drinking water are readily accessible. Canada is seen as a strong and stable democratic nation and an international defender of human rights, including the freedom to enact fundamental change to create fairer and more just systems of government. As Prime Minister, I would want to maintain Canada's international standing and reputation.

We have to continue to make strong efforts to welcome people from throughout the world. We must have a more open immigration policy. Canada must continue to be a land of opportunity and hope. We should welcome people from throughout the world as we did 500 years ago in the spirit of peaceful coexistence and sharing the land.

Globalization and the reduction of trade barriers are worldwide phenomena. Canada must improve its position and become a leader in the creation and advancement of appropriate technologies. Advancing our position in the global marketplace in a manner that is both equitable and respectful of the economic and political realities facing our trading partners would be the cornerstone of international trade policy. My government would not take unfair advantage of the developmental needs and poverty plaguing other countries. As well, respect for the rights of local and indigenous peoples, and the political accords they hold with their governments, would be a paramount consideration in all economic relationships.

We must create markets that honour the world's resources, both natural and human. Canada must take the lead in developing international trade policy that redefines economic growth to be responsible, visionary, and sustainable. Canada's international trade policy must embrace a stewardship approach to utilization and reliance both upon our ecosystems and natural resources and upon those of our trade partners. For example, to restore our common environment and protect our common future, we must collaborate with other countries to protect forests and river systems throughout the world.

For me, the future of Canada first requires putting Canada's house in order. This begins with maintaining the commitment to deficit reduction, reducing the ratio of debt to the gross domestic product. But I am also looking at balance. Deficit reduction must never be at the expense of social and environmental programming. For example, I think that these concepts need to be dealt with in a way that more explicitly acknowledges competing demands and more accurately reflects the reality of our society. For example, I would incorporate all of the country's assets and liabilities in describing Canada's financial position. This would mean the value of renewable and non-renewable natural resources, the unpaid contribution of women working at home, the value of parks and pristine lands, these would all be included as assets. The real costs of economic development, including environmental degradation, pollution and clean-up, and the loss of species, habitats, and ecosystem would have to be included. With this approach, Canada's true progress can be measured, and equitable and appropriate decisions for deficit reduction can be made.

The future also resides in our collective ability to meet the challenges of the 21st century head on, with a skilled, highly educated workforce. As a fundamental component of its domestic policy, my government would make a massive investment in training and education for all people—anyone who wanted to be educated would have the right to be educated. Our most important resource, and indeed our future, depends upon our full realization of the enormous potential of Canada's peoples.

Ultimately, the security of Canada depends upon our government's ability to ensure stability to Canadians—those who live, work, and deserve to prosper here. Thus, a critical focus of domestic policy should be directed at the creation of meaningful, evolutionary, satisfying employment opportunities. One can reasonably ask how one would create jobs that meet these criteria. An infusion of resources into locally based economies would maintain the security and future of the many small, rural communities that characterize much of our vast country. In my government, these resources would be secured through adjustments to current priorities and a more equitable tax system that obligates those with the greatest ability to pay their fair share.

As Prime Minister, I would be cognizant of the need to address the entire range of the responsibilities of office and the interests of all Canadians. Prosperity, unity, and a strong position in the global economy are national requirements for any Prime Minister. But one national requirement that deserves particular priority is the unmet need to restore dignity, hope, and a viable future to First Nations.

The Anishinabe, and the many other indigenous peoples of Canada, have suffered disenfranchisement, legislated assimilation, and economic marginalization within Canada. These are facts of history. They confer upon us a legacy of problems—not just for Anishinabe but for Canadians. This legacy is brought to our attention in the annual reports of the Canadian Human Rights Commission— the conditions of indigenous peoples remain the most serious human rights problem in Canada. It is the legacy of impoverishment and underdevelopment of a segment of Canadian society and it has become too costly for any Prime Minister to ignore.

The costs to Canada are many. The reports of the Canadian Human Rights Commission, as well as many other commissions of inquiry, are themselves a source of great embarrassment to Canada internationally. A country with such wealth and stability must clearly demonstrate its ability to be fair and just to all its citizens.

There are also very direct costs. With poverty comes an array of community, environmental, social, health, family, and individual problems. We see the outcome in highly disproportionate utilization or representation of Aboriginal people in the justice system, the healthcare system, the social services system, and the welfare system. These are huge and unproductive costs that do not address the issue, or even cope with the problems.

But the greatest costs are the lost opportunities that result from failing to develop the human resources and economies of the hundreds of vibrant communities and many diverse cultures of First Nations in Canada. There is no reason for us to continue to fail in this area. Canada has the capacity and the national interest to support necessary development of First Nations. What is required is the will to do it. As Prime Minister, I would have the will.

Canada's priority in relation to First Nations would be to support the development of productive, sustainable economies. This would not mean just another economic development program from the Department of Indian Affairs. What are required are an across-the-board commitment and participation from the various sectors of the Government of Canada.

It would mean, for example, that the Minister of Indian Affairs and the Minister of Human Resource Development would immediately place social-programming resources under First Nations control and support investment in innovative and productive training and employment programs.

It would also mean that the Minister of Health and Welfare would be fully committed to ensuring that both service aspects and business aspects of First Nations health care were fully in support of community economies. Health care is a huge industry that has yet to provide economic benefits to First Nations. This would be accomplished by placing healthcare programs and resources in First Nations control.

I would want to ensure that the policies and programs of the minister of Justice and the Solicitor General were absolutely compatible and supportive of developing a First Nations system of justice. The consensus of numerous commissions of inquiry is that Canada's justice system has failed Aboriginal people and that the solutions to the problem lie in community-based institutions for policing, sentencing, restorative justice, and corrections. I would want to see the development of these institutions. This means jobs for people who will be committed to a justice system that works in the interests of their community.

For the various ministries with responsibilities in environment, lands, and resources, I would want to see a comprehensive and integrated strategy for ensuring that First Nations benefit equitably from land and resource use. This would involve initiatives as diverse as settlement of land claims, development of First Nations capacity in environmental assessment and the management of resource development; or, supporting the development of institutional arrangements for cooperative management of lands and resources. This means employment in communities whose traditions of wise environmental stewardship are legendary worldwide.

As Prime Minister, I would look beyond government to the private sector for the real engine of economic development for First Nations. But government can help in building a bridge between the First Nations and corporate communities. For example, government funds in areas such as housing, public facilities, and community infrastructure are insufficient to meet the current needs of First Nations. But government programs do provide a stable and reliable cash flow. This is just what a lending institution wants to see. Government funding can leverage a much larger investment fund for building and developing the communities and economies that will sustain First Nations in the future.

As Prime Minister, I would be very conscious of the need for broad public understanding, respect, and support for First Nations development. There must be an understanding that such development is in everyone's interest. It is investing in Canada through the renewal of productive communities. But surveys reveal appalling levels of misinformation among Canadians concerning First Nations living conditions, access to public funds, and capacity for self-government. I believe that Canada has permitted a dangerous degree of ignorance to remain unaddressed. Our inaction sustains ideas and attitudes that have no place in Canada today. I would want to ensure that public education on First Nations matters were given due priority as a national issue and that First Nations people were the educators. More employment for those best qualified.

It goes without saying that as Prime Minister I would stand behind Canada's commitments and obligations to honour the treaty and aboriginal rights of First Nations—including the inherent right of self-government. I would want to see expeditious implementation of self-government arrangements, such as the initiative in Manitoba whereby we, through our process, will create a third order of government: First Nations government. This profound initiative will have the effect of restoring jurisdictions to First Nations, creating structures of government to give effect to these jurisdictions, and dismantling the Department of Indian Affairs. The new or renewed structures of First Nations government, together with developed economies, employment and control over public programs and services, will allow First Nations to take their own lead in enriching and revitalizing their cultures, communities, and Canada.

As a final fundamental point, unity is critical to the future well-being of Canada. There can be no greater strength to Canada than to see a society that respects the differences that exist among its peoples, in its languages, cultures, values, and histories, and to thrive and build on this diversity. We are one people, one country.

A Call for Reform: Governments Must Concentrate on What They Do Best

MONIQUE JÉRÔME-FORGET

MONIQUE JÉRÔME-FORGET

Monique Jérôme-Forget is President of the Institute for Research on Public Policy in Montreal. She holds a doctorate in psychology from McGill University and served as president of the Quebec Workers Compensation Board and the Occupational Health and Safety Commission and as an assistant deputy minister at Health and Welfare Canada. During her academic career, Dr. Jérôme-Forget worked at McGill as an adjunct professor (1990–91) and at Concordia University, where she was vice-rector from 1985 to 1986. She is a member of Statistics Canada's Chief Statistician's Advisory Council and a director on numerous boards, including the Canada Life Assurance Company, the McGill Institute for the Study of Canada, the Social Sciences and Humanities Research Council, la Société d'investissement jeunesse, Premier Choix: TVEC Inc., and the Quebec Advisory Board of SHL Systemhouse. She has represented Canada at several international congresses, and is actively involved in supporting the music and theatre communities in Montreal.

No effective public policy can be fashioned in Canada without reference to a key, indeed fundamental, change in the way the public views government. That must be the starting point for any Prime Minister engaged in determining what must be done to prepare the country for the next century.

It is inescapably true that the mood in the country has changed. Citizens are wary of big, centralized government. They demand greater accountability, more flexibility, more choice. They are tired of inefficient, bloated bureaucracies. They are fed up with gaping deficits, high taxes, and declining services. In short, there is real anger in the land; and the amount of anger that Ottawa is generating means something is manifestly wrong.

The question of accountability must be addressed if we are to make any progress in improving the situation. I would ensure that government responsibilities—provincial and federal particularly—do not overlap, since citizens must be able to point to those who develop policies that do not suit them. I would clearly separate levels of responsibility and devolve as much as possible to governments closest to the people.

Second, the services left to governments must be delivered more efficiently. I would seek to develop agencies based on the model of the United Kingdom, where accountability rests with those responsible for policy development and the administration of programs. Crucial to this idea is the concept of a Citizen's Charter, which lays out the standards by which citizens should be served and the redress they may seek if dissatisfied. Third, I would use my influence to appropriate greater powers to improve the state of the economic union. These are the three main keys of my approach.

To see why these remedies are necessary, it is useful to reflect on the changes we have lived through in recent times. The 1960s and 1970s in Canada, as indeed in other countries, were decades of centralization and big government. Unfashionable as it is today to assert it, those years produced much of value, not only in countries with a strong, interventionist tradition, but even in more laisser-faire places, not least the United States. They also created a strong attachment between citizens and the government; many of us shared the values of the Great Society, and supported the idea of government action to strike a fairer balance between efficiency and equity.

Since then, following the wild expansion of deficits, the increasing globalization of investment and trade, and a decline in the quality of services, governments have found their room for action hopelessly straitened. Central governments can no longer afford to bestride their national economies, pouring funds into ever more generous social programs and dictating investment and trade flows through edict, direct interference, and hamstrung rules and regulations.

The declining autonomy of national governments and the fissures in the social contract generated by this loss of autonomy have led to loud calls for a more responsive politics, a reflection of citizens' views not just on the basis of the "national interest" (which, in any event, is increasingly difficult to define) but on a regional or even local basis. A prescription for the next 10 years would cluster around two key themes: accountability and decentralization. Who is responsible? People want to know whom to blame when things go wrong. But it is not enough in a country of Canada's size, development, and prospects merely to insist on a measure of direct accountability between politician and civil servant on the one hand and the citizen-consumer on the other. In order to maximize accountability, there needs to be a clear separation of political powers and, in the Canadian context, that requires rethinking the relationship between the federal government and the provinces.

There is already a large and influential literature about the advantages of decentralization. Alice Rivlin's[1] work is an example: she argues that regions are better at running the show than are central governments, chiefly because they are more attuned to local needs and more supple in their policy responses.

But the key text of recent years has been *Reinventing Government*, by David Osborne and Ted Gaebler,[2] who coined the by-now hackneyed, but no less crucial, concept of steering rather than rowing. Governments ought to be more concerned with policy development than with program administration. They ought to concentrate on the things they do well, rather than on the broad range of activities that for so long characterized the ascribed duties of big government.

This approach is convincing partly because it accords so well with the shifting views of citizens, as evinced in recent elections in Canada, the United States, France, and even in many countries in the developing world.

Voters in Canada, as in other countries, increasingly want a say in the direction that society and the economy move in, and there is a great pressure to devolve power out from the centre to facilitate this. The trend could have the subsidiary, and quite laudable, effect of increasing the attachment of citizens to their communities. If there is more responsive government, civil society as a whole benefits. There is, after all, a great need for a revival of civics in most developed countries. The lack of community spirit in many of our cities and large towns is depressingly common and has had detrimental consequences. The penetrating work of Robert Putnam[3] makes this point eloquently.

For the federal government, the lessons in all of this are obvious. Ottawa ought to encourage a devolution of powers. It should devolve to the provinces, returning to them the role they had—at least since the 1930s—in creating, developing, and implementing social and economic policies. Such an approach presupposes a strong commitment to democracy, to the idea that voters in the regions have every right to elect politicians with different and even opposing views.

To make decentralization work, we must open the door wider to asymmetry. Not every province need make identical policy choices, nor provide the same basket of services. Particularly, in the name of accountability, we should respect diversity. In the United States, for instance, Maine differs from Florida, Florida differs from Wyoming. In Canada, the West is different, Quebec is different, the Maritimes are different, and so is Ontario, of course; our theories and practices of governance ought to reflect this diversity and support it.

The traditional argument against decentralization has always been the need to ensure equity. Without a strong central government, it is said, there would too much regional disparity and too many barriers to mobility in a country built on the concept of basic freedoms—not least of movement.

Any sensible discussion of decentralization must confront this issue. I am not arguing in favour of dropping all norms across the country. A federation ought to have some basic standards, of course, and these have been and can continue to be developed jointly. For instance, there is a need for minimum health and safety regulations, and definitive rules for labelling of food and drugs.

More crucially, we cannot lose the basic freedoms of a federal democracy; mobility, for instance, must be protected. But ought the government services delivered everywhere be identical? Surely not. There is no possible way to ensure that services in Toronto are going to be equivalent to those in the Îles-de-la-Madeleine. Standards have never been the same across the country, nor will they ever be.

And why should one expect the same benefits all over? I challenge that. If we move from one state to another, do we expect the same services? Local needs, provincial needs, regional needs must be acknowledged. Day care need not and never will be identical across the country. In Quebec, we might go for one form that is partially subsidized and basically run by parents. Ontario has opted to extend the elementary school system. Alberta wants to have an open system. Canadians ought to accept this diversity and allow innovation.

Similarly, there should be greater flexibility in healthcare delivery. The Quebec government wanted to introduce some user charges for people who make use of the emergency room when it is not strictly necessary. The provincial government wanted to channel people into local community service centres, to take the pressure off emergency services. That policy contravened the *Canada Health Act* and will never be implemented. Should one not be made to pay for the self-selected service of emergency care in cases in which it is not truly warranted?

The various strategies chosen by different jurisdictions have even greater value than simply their service to the citizens in question. It is one of my central contentions that innovation is one of the very best side effects of the flexible approach I am advocating. Provinces (even cities and regions) ought to be encouraged to try new things. Innovation can lead to creative approaches, and these could prove very useful to other jurisdictions. Experimentation across the country is like creating a series of incubators that can foment the development of excellent policy strategies. Once they work in one province, for example, they can be picked up elsewhere. This is an attractive way of making a virtue out of our differences.

Centralized standards taken to extremes can stifle innovation and make it impossible to meet local needs and respond to local choices. No government ought to make the choice between community centres and hospitals. These choices belong to citizens and citizens also vote at the provincial level.

What about the competitive "dumping" of welfare cases? This is a criticism often levelled against those who argue in favour of decentralization. I grant that there is no point in Alberta "dumping" its welfare cases onto British Columbia—if such a thing ever really happened. There must be room for some form of harmonization. But we have proven equal to the task in the past of developing some standards for programs, and can continue to do so collectively.

With a few exceptions, the federal government ought to concentrate on the economic union and leave social policy in the hands of lower levels of government—which can more directly respond to the needs of those who elect them.

Ottawa has a central duty to concentrate on controlling the deficit (as most provinces have already succeeded in doing). There is also a need to push for harmonization on economic issues (trade, investment, and so on). For instance, the government was surely right to try to create the centralized Securities and Exchange Commission, to unite the work of the British Columbia, Alberta, Quebec, and Ontario authorities. The Canadian stock market is simply too small to be dealt with regionally, and it puts us at a disadvantage vis-à-vis other jurisdictions (especially the United States) if we fragment and balkanize the market. Quebec and British Columbia both said no. They were wrong. The federal government ought to pursue this idea vigorously, as it is precisely the sort of policy best promoted by the central government in a federation.

More generally, Ottawa must also ensure there is economic cohesion in the country and that economic policy is framed in the best interests of all citizens. One of the key problems concerns the fact that Canadian economic life is mostly linked to Central Canada and if Southern Ontario overheats, our monetary policy is geared to addressing that problem, despite any detrimental effect on other regions of the country. In addition, the policy that calls upon equalization payments to ensure economic cohesion is not without a cost. Consequently, the rich provinces feel that they need all their wealth to compete internationally. This transfer also gives the illusion that provinces are equally treated.

Beyond the need to limit and sometime increase Ottawa's powers, good governance implies efficient and effective governments. In general, governments should concentrate exclusively on what they do best and should devolve power to agencies, thus allowing true experimentation across the regions.

The agency model is a new way of devolving power and improving accountability in government. The United Kingdom, Australia, and New Zealand have been successfully experimenting with the concept.

The agency approach means setting up separate divisions providing government services. The theory is that ministers should think about policies, not day-to-day operations. The crucial first step is to determine which services must be delivered by government and which could more profitably and efficiently be farmed out to private-sector players. The next step is to reform the remaining service-delivery mechanisms to ensure that they respond to citizen-client demand, and that services are efficiently delivered by fully accountable agents.

The British experience is revealing in this regard. Following the publication of the Ibbs Report in 1988, the Next Steps executive agency model was proposed, leading for the first time to the separation of policy formulation from operational responsibilities. This had the effect of ensuring that the government would steer, rather than row, using the power of the marketplace and the attendant accountability it generates to determine the most efficient allocation of scarce resources and the targetting of services to those who really need them. By this spring, Britain had created 125 agencies, representing more than 70 percent of the public sector.[4] Crucially, the agency model was accompanied by a Citizen's Charter. This clearly laid out the targets set by agencies for a range of government services. These range from the amount of time it takes to process a passport application to the efficiency of the motor vehicles branch in Swansea.

Moreover, there was a real mechanism in place for citizens (as consumers of public services) to complain and, in a few instances, to receive compensation in the event that their needs were not met. For example, any delay on London's Underground of longer than 15 minutes results in a refund. This is true accountability. A Citizen's Charter, in my view, would give Canadians a way to get back at governments for poor services.

In Canada, sadly, the experience became politicized. The previous administration made a timid attempt to introduce special operating agencies in 1990, but managed to set up only 15 by 1993, covering just three percent of the civil service.[5] The incoming Liberal government cancelled the program, following a negative (and, to my mind, misguided) report by the Auditor General. In the end, we were left with the status quo, a multi-layered hierarchical bureaucracy without clear rules for accountability.

The agency approach should be introduced nationally and provincially. In order to succeed, the government needs to ensure that it appoints a sponsoring leader—a "mentor"—who will work to ensure that the system is implemented and developed widely.

I dwell on the agency model because it provides a concrete example of how to render government more accountable. But it is only one step in a much larger process of reforming government, which must emphasize democratic accountability throughout the civil service, a fair and efficient sharing of political power between the centre and the regions, and respect for the needs and desires of citizens.

It is not an easy time to be Prime Minister of a country as large, as diverse, and, in many ways, as muddled as Canada. The old certainties are gone, burned in the blaze of globalization, still onerous, debt, and the soured relationship between the governing and the governed.

But there are ways forward, as I have attempted to convey here. The first step must be to recognize the end of the old orthodoxies of big government once and for all. We must then determine just how to devolve power downward, so that it resides as close as possible to the citizens to whom politicians owe their jobs, and to whom they must be accountable. Decentralization is not one option among many for a country such as Canada, at a time such as this. It is a necessity.

Finally, as a way of achieving the accountability so crucial in a modern nation-state we must look at every opportunity to tap the expertise of the marketplace to generate greater efficiency. The agency model is a satisfying, even elegant answer to the conundrum, "How do we provide for the public good, efficiently, reliably, and equitably, within the constraints of a modern, open and global economy?" We owe it to ourselves to answer the question.

Notes

1. Alice M. Rivlin, *Reviving the American Dream: The Economy, the States, and the Federal Government* (Washington, DC: The Brookings Institution, 1992).
2. David Osborne and Ted Gaebler, *Reinventing Government: How the Entrepreneurial Spirit is Transforming the Public Sector* (Reading, MA: Addison-Wesley Publishing Company, fourth printing, April 1992).
3. Robert D. Putnam, Bowling Alone: America's Declining Social Capital, *Journal of Democracy* (volume 6, number 1, January 1995), pages 65–78.
4. U.S. Cabinet Office, Next Steps Briefing Note, pages 5 and 9.
5. Peter Aucoin, Operational Agencies: From Half-Hearted Efforts to Full-fledged Government Reform, *Choices* (volume 2, number 4, April 1996), page 8.

Constructive Destruction
Will Let in the Future

FRANK OGDEN

FRANK OGDEN

Known as "Dr. Tomorrow," futurist Frank Ogden lives on his high-tech houseboat in Vancouver harbour. A best-selling author, business consultant, and speaker, Mr. Ogden helped found Canada's first think tank, the Synectics Foundation, and was a founding member of the Canadian chapter of the World Future Society. In 1989, he was elected a Fellow of the Explorers Club, an elite group of adventurers that includes mountaineer Sir Edmund Hillary and astronaut John Glenn. From his Vancouver houseboat, Mr. Ogden conducted the world's first two international seminars via satellite and fibre-optic technology. His latest books, *The Last Book You'll Ever Read* and *Navigating in Cyberspace*, present visions of a radically different future including the advent of human cyborgs. He has been profiled on numerous television and radio shows as well as in newspapers and magazines around the world.

If I were Prime Minister, to improve living standards and unite this country, I wouldn't do what everyone else has been trying to do unsuccessfully for 130 years by leaning on sentiment, patriotism, and nationalism. I would let the country fracture and then from the pieces assemble an assortment of regions that wanted to belong instead of trying to patch up parties in an unworkable divorce. We have had enough of politicians, bureaucrats, and people whose income levels depend on maintaining the status quo and manipulating the population to their views. Those days are gone. Weren't Meech Lake and the Constitution debate a clear enough answer? Constructive destruction has its place.

In my opinion, everyone—individuals, small companies, corporations, and countries—should take a reality check at least once every 130 years. So on this Canada Day 1996, I say:

If I were Prime Minister, first I would step back and cool down. Then I would take a non-political, non-patriotic, non-nationalistic look at our country. I did. And what I see and sense, from my somewhat unique perspective, is a country that doesn't work.

It once did. I didn't spend six years in the Royal Canadian Air Force during World War II just for laughs while doing the ultimate— laying my life on the line for my country. I wouldn't do it today. I am not alone.

Under the United Nations charter, people are supposedly free to determine their own destiny—free to select the type of country in which they want to live and the type of government they want to govern them. Same applies in a Canadian democracy, especially since our Constitution contains no appropriate legal wording on how to achieve separation. Just do it, as the phrase goes. While this is fine in theory, it is not easy in practice. Look at Hong Kong. Canada differs only in the more sophisticated methods used. Has anyone in Canada beyond Quebec even suggested a referendum on the separation issue for the rest of us? Has anybody asked us who we want to live with?

A country is like a family. Eventually, the offspring want to do their own thing. They want to find independence as they see it, which as most parents grow to realize, is more often than not radically different from the result they originally intended. Only then can they obtain by learning—not being taught—the self-confidence required for survival. At no time has this been easy. Some don't make it, although eventually the majority succeed. When they do, it's a confidence you'll never find staying home.

When the United Nations was created in 1948, there were only 50 countries on the planet. Now there are that many in Africa. The United Nations currently lists 185 countries and the list is growing. Does anyone really believe that such a growth rate—a new country almost every four months over the last 48 years on average—is an accident? Let's get a grip.

When I was a kid, the only satellite in the sky was the moon. It wasn't until 1945 that visionary author Arthur C. Clarke (*2001: A Space Odyssey*) created the concept of artificial satellites. As soon as these new satellites started circling the skies, the world changed. Satellites fail to recognize national boundaries. This had never happened before. A little robot showed us. The world changed. Take a look.

When a river changes course, sailing the old route doesn't work. A ship's engine can work a thousand times harder but with no resulting movement. It was designed for a different environment. The course of Canada has been altered. Since the early days of Sputnik and Alouette, the new communications environment has been producing a solvent that is dissolving the ties that bound countries together in the past. The United Nations will soon have 250 members. What makes you think 20th-century Canada will still be one of them?

At one time, community meant a strictly specific geographical area where people of similar interests gathered to live and work. Today, thousands of new communities exist, work, and live on the Internet and World Wide Web. Hundreds are added daily. They are the fastest growing communities on the planet. The first electronic communities could only communicate via text. Still images and sound quickly developed. Weeks later, black-and-white video. Today, colour. Now anyone can videoconference from anywhere to anywhere on the planet—for about $1 an hour! I've been doing it for more than a year.

The world has changed. Some already see cyberspace as their sovereign state. Once upon a time you could say such a bizarre idea would never happen. Like when people said they would never deal with a robot—then found themselves lining up to use an automated banking machine. Just like what many said about putting satellites in space, going to the moon, or having a heart transplant. Remember that in times of chaos, panic, and rapid change, the bizarre rapidly becomes acceptable.

This is today's reality. The world is not the same place with the same emotions, ideals and idols, concepts and compliance, mass markets or mass think that we knew 20, 10, five, a year, or even a week ago. As humankind globalizes, humankind tribalizes. More than 100,000 high-paying jobs, connected with these new Internet communications links, will be created this year alone and many more in 1997. Where are you putting your energies and brain power? In the past or in the future? Holding together 19th-century dreams or creating your own modern ones?

Recent World Bank figures, under its new method of calculation, show Australia and Canada as the world's richest countries. But according to the World Bank, in both countries this wealth is 80 percent inherited. It came with the land, forests, minerals, and fish in the sea. Only 20 percent came from developing brain power.

Japan's situation is just the reverse. Eighty percent of its wealth comes from brain power, only 20 percent from natural resources. Even the United States has a better balance than Canada or Australia. Sixty percent of American wealth comes from brain power, only 40 percent from natural resources.

And what does the future offer? Less dependency everywhere on what have been in the past our most lucrative natural resources. Ninety percent of all the goods and services that we will interact with a decade from now haven't yet been developed. Most will involve new materials and techniques not available currently.

If we persist in producing only what developing countries now produce, we will only generate Third World wages as economies go global. If we can only compete with those kids in Karachi, we will only make what they make. And at the speed that many Asian countries and economies are moving, they may still end up eating our lunch.

Governments, as we have known them, no longer can do what they were set up to do. Like protect citizens at home or abroad. Name any country that can protect citizens against terrorism. What country can protect the value of its currency? Not even Japan. Who can

protect the jobs of their citizens? And importing labour—photonical-
ly—hasn't even hit Main Street yet.

What country has been able to throw up a protective shield
against unwanted and illegal immigrants? Who can stop cultural
degradation from washing over their borders? If a country can't
enforce a law, rule, sanction, or embargo everywhere, it can't enforce
it anywhere. This failure to perform also applies to almost any
Industrial Age institution.

The wealthiest countries on this earth, with little or no debt, are
the smallest—exactly the opposite of most national situations during
the faded Industrial Age.

In round figures, each Canadian owes, through his or her share of
national and provincial debt, about $30,000. In a future that will be
capital intensive—not labour intensive—this is not the required condition for the fat and lazy to be in during the gruelling global economic contest rising on the horizon. Also, don't be too surprised to
see some demanding a political crimes tribunal to handle politicians
who promised one thing and delivered another. A new sense of
accountability can change the whole picture. Look what a revolution
did for France. Keep remembering: in times of chaos, panic, and rapid
change, the bizarre can instantly become acceptable.

As Prime Minister, I'd say, "Forget the past. Let people vote on
particular referendums of their choice and then work towards well-
defined futures under whatever various labels we decide, instead of
spending untold years and fortunes trying to hold together a past
dream of destiny, something already basically beyond our control."

Perhaps if all provinces and territories separate, we could then
recombine in a new collaborative family made up of thinking and
considerate cousins instead of bickering siblings. Perhaps something
along the lines of what the 23 states of Switzerland have produced
and profited from for the past 700 years, or that which 21st-century
Spain is now attempting.

Think about education. Global communications is going to
change everything. Consider why we need to have classes with expensive teachers telling us about Paris when any 10-year-old can, in minutes, contact, talk to—and see—his e-mail pal there and get the latest

correct information direct, for $1 an hour? In Singapore schooling isn't even compulsory, yet everyone wants to go to school. Why?

Consider welfare. Why do we deny people survival and learning and working experiences? The current method hasn't worked for the 50 years I've been watching.

I see the least unemployment, least national and personal debt, and greatest wealth generators in countries with the lowest taxes and where the private sector pays taxes for doing at lower cost most of what we have allocated to high-cost governments. Look around. The countries with people producing efficiently, utilizing the latest technology, have low unemployment, rising incomes, most of which they keep. They can afford the best medical treatment, modern transportation, and a constantly upgraded infrastructure. We aren't doing it well anymore and as soon as we realize that our rigidity and resistance to change are part of the problem half the solution has already appeared.

Prime Ministers should tell the truth, as they see it—and this is mine.

Take it From Me:
I Learned the Hard Way

BOB RAE

BOB RAE

Bob Rae served as Premier of Ontario from 1990 to 1995, and was elected eight times to federal and provincial parliaments before his retirement from politics in 1996. He led the New Democratic Party of Ontario from 1982 to 1996 and served as Leader of the Official Opposition before becoming Premier. Mr. Rae has a Bachelor of Arts and a Bachelor of Laws from the University of Toronto, and was a Rhodes Scholar from Ontario in 1969. He obtained a Master of Philosophy degree from Oxford University in 1971 and was named a Queen's Counsel in 1984. He is also an adjunct professor at the University of Toronto in the faculties of Law, Management, and Arts and Science. Mr. Rae is a partner at the Canadian international law firm of Goodman Phillips & Vineberg.

The first thing I would do as Prime Minister is draw up a short list of lessons from my time as Premier of Ontario. Do fewer things better. Attract the best people and give them clearly assigned jobs. Focus my own time and make sure I'm taking enough time off and away to be able to use my energy better. Set goals and targets and meet them. Govern every day with the knowledge that the public's trust and confidence can change on a dime; earning it back is always more difficult—the public will forgive an excess of humility more readily than arrogance.

The first issue facing the Prime Minister of Canada today is the country itself. There is no point pretending this is not a problem. It cannot be wished away. The timetable for a future provincial referendum in Quebec is out of my hands, but that does not make me powerless. I would not make "concessions" to Quebec, but would rather urge Mr. Bouchard to present in detail his plan for the future partnership between Quebec and the rest of Canada.

This plan should be considered carefully by the rest of the country. If it is rejected as the basis for negotiation, reasons should be stated clearly, and the alternatives presented to the people of Quebec and the people of Canada. We cannot leave all the initiative with the Quebec government, since that puts the rest of Canada in the position of constantly making concessions toward Quebec without any assurance that any of these will produce a lasting settlement.

I would, at the same time, make a strong case to the people of Quebec about why the country should stay together, and why the association called federalism makes sense for them and for all of us. We have been cleaning our constitutional glasses in Canada for a long time. It is an endless process that baffles and annoys most Canadians. It is also entirely inadequate for the task at hand. If we do not recognize Quebec as a distinct society within Canada, Quebec will insist on being treated as a distinct society outside Canada. We must make the structure of a new confederation generous and flexible enough to include all the partners, all the regions of the country, and all the people of Canada. Above all, we must get on with it.

We cannot afford a 10- or 15-year divorce proceeding. The world will pass us by. Old formulas will not keep us together. In the end, we shall accept what stares us in the face: Canada requires sharing and division of power, of sovereignty. The provinces are sovereign in some areas; federal institutions in others. The world is interdependent. No sovereignty is absolute. We shall relearn these truths and make them our own. We shall have to reinvent and re-create Canada.

Think of those things we have in common. First, there is the land we share. Imagine for a moment the first trip up the Saguenay by Europeans, the first view of Lake Ontario, Lake Superior, Niagara. Go north from the cities huddled along the rivers and lakes near the American border. See the Canada we share. In the embarrassingly self-conscious poetic preamble to the *Act Respecting the Future of Quebec* (1995), there is talk of "winter" as if this belongs only to Quebec. Not so; we are partners in weather as well as geography. That is why we both go to Florida. The landscape that inspires Quebeckers inspires the rest of us as well. It is the same.

We are not conquerors. There is none among us now. The battle for domination in North America between two European empires is over. Behind us. None of us alive today was there among the foreign troops. Let's stop pretending we were. There is a history to be learned and respected. There is also a mythology from which we must awaken.

The reconciliation must include Native Canadians as well. For centuries our legal and political systems pretended Canada's first people were invisible. Our culture and folklore pretended they were savages. This, too, is a history we must now change.

The challenges we face are common challenges. Living and working in a global economy requires teamwork and partnership for us to succeed. A shared challenge of creating good jobs for a new generation, a need to maintain a decent social order, and to keep the sense of our having common obligations for "peace, order, and good government" despite the pressures of the world upon us.

Of course, unity cannot be the only preoccupation. In fact, we must become more outward-looking than we are today. We are an international country, and indeed our identity is ever increasingly connected to the global society around us. More than most places in the world, we make our way as a country by making products better than others, of better quality, and at a better price. Yet that is not all we are. We are sustained by a healthy economy, and this economy in turn builds a stronger society.

Efficiency and justice are not enemies. Productivity, fairness, and sustainability are not incompatible. In fact, they need each other to build the kind of Canada we want. As Prime Minister, I would focus my attention on the need to reconcile these core values of our society. For too long a time, we have forgotten the need for productivity and efficiency in our economy and our public finances. We should not make the mistake of forgetting the need for social justice and environmental sustainability as we correct the first problem.

We need: a national plan for greater productivity and, in particular a tax system that will promote just that; a stronger agreement on national standards, particularly for health care, social services, and education; a coordinated approach to debt reduction and fiscal management; and a new common attack on poverty among our children and their families.

By a "national plan," I certainly do not mean something imposed from on high by Ottawa. Ottawa has to adjust to a world where it will have less unilateral power. It is ironic that Ottawa's real economic power was reduced during the Trudeau era more than in any other, but that is a simple reflection of the fact that Mr. Trudeau did not focus clearly enough on the need for a strong, balanced economy. Ottawa can only work in partnership with the provinces and all the other social and economic forces in our society.

This partnership, like all human endeavours, needs focus and leadership. This is what a Prime Minister and his team can provide. But it can only really work as a team, that includes provincial governments as well as business, labour, and the broader community.

On taxes, we have been bedevilled by the fruitless debate between those who want the tax system to redistribute wealth and those who believe it should only reward success. In fact, we want the tax system to do two basic things: to raise revenue fairly, and to promote growth and national goals such as more jobs and more investment in human capital. We need to be more creative about how this can be done. Taxes on employment are counter-productive. At the same time, we should be rewarding speculation less and real investment in people more. I would invite the social partners to discuss how this can be done. I also believe that lower interest rates are just as important as lower taxes, and there is no point in keeping deficits and interest rates high at the same time we keep lowering taxes in the name of "relief." This is not relief. This is just trading a headache for an upset stomach.

Lower payroll taxes; increase tax credits for job creation and for investments in training and research and development; match taxes on consumption with reduced income taxes on the less well-off to ensure that fairness and progressivity are maintained. Continue to provide incentives for employee ownership and worker participation. Give everyone a stake in the success of the national enterprise. Keep the whole thing flatter and simpler, and insist on more cooperation with the provinces. The current duplication and turf warfare are not helping.

I would bring the social partners together to insist that we set national (that is, federal and provincial) standards on health care, social services, and education. We're actually making good progress here, but we should keep it up. We have to do more to share best practices, to introduce efficiencies, and to maintain the good access and quality in health care that are, in fact, a strength for Canada. We are a better society and a better economy for having the social systems we have. Don't throw them away. Fix them in cooperation with the provinces. Our welfare systems need to be more proactive. Work and training need more emphasis. We need to engage our teachers, students, and parents in a common effort to give Canada the best education in the world.

Debt matters. Believe me, I had to learn the hard way. We all carry about with us certain pictures in our heads. When I was a kid, television was in its infancy. We really did gather around to watch "Leave it to Beaver" and "Father Knows Best." I grew up in a world where Canada had a national economy and the assumption of strong central government to go with it. There was steady economic growth, with rising incomes and low levels of private and public debt. It was a Canada firmly based on industry and resources, with a labour force that was largely white, male, and working a traditional 40-hour week and a narrowing gap between rich and poor. This was a world where people "knew their place." Most women stayed at home. Single-income, two-parent families were the norm. Voting patterns were reasonably stable.

Between 1945 and 1975, life improved for everyone in Canada and Ontario, with very few exceptions. The steelworker factories that I used to visit as a young advocate for the United Steelworkers had tens of thousands of workers (as opposed to a few thousand now), who could all point to their own experience as living proof that collective action and positive government policy had in fact improved their lives.

We live in a world of fewer certainties today. The rising tide of economic growth has lifted some boats, but others have capsized and sunk. Both in the United States and in Canada, more wealth is now owned and controlled by fewer people. Many working people are clinging to the life-rafts. People have gone into debt to support a standard of living that they feel they need and deserve, and that they clearly see others, no more meritorious than they, enjoying and even flaunting. Governments have done the same thing.

We now live not so much in a national economy as in a series of regional economies increasingly linked to global interdependence. A closed economy is a figment of the political imagination. It does not exist. It cannot be willed into existence. Sovereignty is not an absolute. Every country in the world that seeks partnerships and associations has had to learn the limits of sovereignty.

Since 1975, we have moved to an even faster-moving information economy. The phrase "global village" was invented in the 1960s. Thirty years later it is closer to a reality. Manufacturing remains critical to our ability to make our way in the world, but even here the key to our success is how we apply new technologies and new techniques to existing processes, how—to use the buzz words—we "add value." The pace of this technological revolution is even more dramatic than the industrial revolution. We are in the middle of it. Its pace is relentless. Its scope is global. We can't stop it. We can only learn how to manage it better, and how to deal with its impact.

Yet the global village is not yet a real community. Some do well. Many more do not. The effect of globalization has been to increase both opportunity and inequality.

In this increasingly polarized world, some people are working longer hours, for which they are well rewarded. Others are not so lucky, forced to accept part-time work when they would vastly prefer more. Women have entered the labour force in unprecedented numbers. Families are being transformed. Canada has become a multiracial country in the space of three decades.

Our world has become disconnected in a number of important ways. The wealth that accrues to the highly skilled and the already rich has less and less to do with the immediate community around it, and much more with the global economy. People have lost their sense of connection between the taxes they pay and the services they receive. In a non-inflationary world, where pay cheques are stagnant or declining, tax increases feel like a direct assault on one's security. The tax revolt we see now is genuine. The left has underestimated its importance and has been slow to learn the difference between what is politically possible in a world with no inflation. Tax increases can no longer be buried in a tide of ever-rising prices and incomes.

There has been much nonsense spouted about the issue of public deficits and public debt, from all sides. This is a practical, and not a theological, question. The public airwaves are dominated by ideological theorists from the left and the right. Many on the left are not prepared to admit that too much public debt is ever a problem. For the right, who are now in the ascendancy, any deficit or debt is a sin. Both views are wrong.

The best explanation I have been able to find for what has happened to all our public finances is that we have used the credit card to maintain the standard of living we believe we need and deserve. Once this started in the early 1970s, it became hard to stop, and compound interest and excessively high interest rates did the rest. This is as true for individuals as it is for governments.

A problem that has taken 25 years to create, in Canada as in most other Western economies, cannot be solved overnight. But it must be solved and cannot be ignored. To deal with it in a balanced way will take determination and judgement. If we overreact, as some governments are clearly doing, more damage will be done by the treatment than by the disease. If we continue to deny the problem, as many on the left still want to do, we are missing a major, changed reality.

The Hippocratic oath reminds doctors to avoid causing unnecessary pain. Governments need to be reminded of this. Governments need, from time to time, like individuals, families, and businesses, to borrow and to invest in the future. There are many circumstances when it is shortsighted not to do so. But just as a family thinks carefully how it will pay down the mortgage or pay off the car loan, governments have to develop a practical sense about how much current income they want to devote to debt-servicing costs. The more that gets eaten up in interest payments, the less there is for everything else, unless economic growth (or lotteries or high taxes) produces more revenue. Here, again, the absence of inflation reveals the arithmetic in its stark nakedness: $10 billion borrowed today is six or seven hundred million dollars required for additional payment tomorrow. That's real money, and it has to come from somewhere.

We also need to distinguish between different kinds of spending. Business accounting makes a distinction between investment and current operations. Governments should do the same. When, for ideological reasons, they fail to make the distinction, necessary investments don't happen. This will affect our competitive position in the future. If investments in mass transit, for example, don't get made, we all pay with congested cities. Yet liveable and affordable cities are key to Canada's economic prosperity.

We need to make sure that all provinces do their accounting the same way and have a set of books that compares with everyone else's. This is not true today. We also need to make sure that our accounts provide good comparisons between capital and operating spending, and give an accurate reflection of the strength of our public assets. We shouldn't be so fixated on our problems that we forget how much public wealth we still have in Canada.

Finally, as Prime Minister, I would recall the progress we have made in the past 30 years on dealing with poverty among older people. We now have to do the same for young children and their families. This will involve a reorganization of both federal and provincial welfare and minimum-wage programs and taxes. Take away all the disincentives against working. Provide a national child benefit, building on the model first proposed in Ontario and now begun in Saskatchewan and British Columbia. Put more attention into education in the early years, as recommended by the Royal Commission on Learning in Ontario.

This is a workable agenda. Its success depends on our coming together as a country, sharing more common goals, and recognizing our common strengths. Wealth creation is a good and necessary thing. But, unless matched by an equal commitment to justice and sustainability, we shall only produce a world where "wealth accumulates and people decay." Canada is a great and good place. It will take all our commitment, all our courage, all our determination to make it grow even stronger and better in the 21st century.

Thinking the Unthinkable, With a Little Help from Plato

PETER KENT

PETER KENT

Born in a Canadian army hospital in Sussex, England, to parents serving with the Canadian Forces during World War II, Peter Kent entered the field of television broadcasting in the early 1960s. His broadcasting career includes stints with several Vancouver radio stations, CTV, and CBC. He anchored CBC's "The National" in the mid 1970s and was a correspondent and host for CBC's "The Journal" in the early 1980s. He has served as a foreign correspondent for NBC in Africa, Central America, and Europe, and was a correspondent and news desk anchor for "World Monitor" out of Boston. He has won numerous awards, including Actras for several CBC documentaries, a Chicago Film Festival Gold for an NBC special on the Middle East, and the Robert F. Kennedy award for a "World Monitor" series on U.S. inner cities. Mr. Kent is a correspondent and news anchor for Global Television News.

Like dregs from fine wine, it's time to decant a little political sludge from the souring vessel of Canadian national unity.

Almost from the day that cave men discovered the mutual benefits of hunting in packs—certainly by the emergence of the first ancient city-state—citizens have struggled with the imperfect relationship of politics and unity. Very often, that relationship has led to the corruption of unity by popular politics.

Approaching the end of the 20th century, Canadians share more than a few of the democratic dilemmas faced by Athenians in the third century BC.

Plato dreamed of a perfect democracy where politicians would be transformed into philosophers. He lamented the essential truth that democracy actually encourages bad leadership—that popular leaders face the constant temptation of maintaining their popularity. (And, as Canadians might recall, even philosopher-politicians can fall victim to that temptation!)

The translator of the most recent version of Plato's Republic, Desmond Lee, reminds those who might dismiss the relevancy of ancient perceptions to contemporary issues that "this is the first generation since [Plato's] when a political leader can address and be seen by the whole electorate."

Of course, television, which has provided today's politicians with that means of communication, has enabled passionate and powerful restatement of the ideals of a united Canada by leaders of most political stripes. (The Parti Québécois and Bloc Québécois use it, contrarily, in the cause of their narrower nationalism.)

At the same time, television has enabled the phenomena that have deepened the cynicism of Canadian citizens in the continuing unity crisis—while, ironically, also enabling the electorate to reject flawed political advice.

One example: the 1992 referendum on the so-called Charlottetown Constitutional Accord, a document of noble intent that was entangled in a web of special interest deals, encased in overwritten legal boiler-plate.

Federal politicians of the day abandoned parliamentary traditions of consideration and debate. While some had the grace to concede great imperfections, they united behind what was described —in somewhat desperate terms—as the last, best deal to save Confederation.

The Charlottetown Accord was promoted with state-financed propaganda, manipulated opinion polls, and scaremongering by influential supporters in the public and private sectors. Early expressions of dissent were dismissed as unpatriotic—even treasonous.

In the end, the electorate refused its consent.

With the wisdom of hindsight, and perhaps a measure of understanding, it is possible to consider the 1992 referendum year as one in which federal politicians "attempted" to put philosophical ideals over partisan politics.

One must also consider, then, the possibility that well-meaning parliamentarians were boondoggled by those who simply wanted to achieve a political end by whatever means necessary. (As happened once before with the repatriation of the Constitution—that remains no small part of our current difficulties!)

There's no question that many of the individual items in the Charlottetown Accord—as in Meech Lake, and countless other proposals before and since—would strengthen the Canadian federation and promote national unity.

Which brings us to the consideration again, in this worthy forum, of the multitude of ideas aimed at revitalizing the country—and keeping it together.

The list of possible improvements is long: any number of constitutional adjustments, the elimination of redundant levels of government, an elected Senate (if a Senate at all), tax reform, the restructuring of social programs, term limits for politicians and senior civil servants (perhaps even CBC journalists), elimination of interprovincial trade barriers, the redress of Aboriginal grievances, redefinition of referendums, and on and on.

But the core problem now, as before, remains the inclination of politicians to play politics even with those ideas from the list above that would be easiest to implement.

With time running out before another federal election (and, inevitably, another referendum on separation in Quebec) it is time to abandon the concept of linkage—buying concensus on unity with deals for special interest groups. As we've seen over the past four decades, national unity achieved with tokenistic federalism does not develop deep roots. Proposals should be considered on their own merits, and either passed into law or put aside.

If this great country is to remain whole, it will be as a result of fair, effective government—not empty promises, intertwined deals, constitutional pork barrelling, or desperate displays of flag-waving affection. (The author remains unconvinced that the positive benefits of the pre-referendum Canada rally in Montreal were greater than the negative one—that the rally might have so offended some *non* voters that they actually cast *oui* votes and made the outcome closer than it would have been!)

Though some Canadian political leaders may still speak the worn platitude that "Quebec separation is unthinkable," it is time for federal, federalist politicians to concede that the break-up of this magnificent dominion is not only "thinkable" but entirely possible.

And if, as a result of opportunities lost in the past few decades, time runs out and a majority of Quebeckers opt for independence, Canadians would have no choice but to accept such a decision. It's too late to change the rules—to set the bar higher. The principle of a 50-percent-plus-one-vote deciding majority has been established by any number of precedents over the past three and a half decades.

The argument that there is no constitutional provision for separation is an empty one. Threats of the forcible maintenance of unity are as anachronistic as the divine right of kings and axe-wielding high executioners.

The cause of unity seems to have been much better served by the sort of spontaneous, "no political strings" support delivered to Quebec's flood-stricken Saguenay region in the summer of 1996. Although impossible to document statistically at the time of this writing, one suspects a significant number of aid recipients have been moved to rethink the ideology of separation as a direct result of the compassionate offerings of ordinary Canadians beyond federal disaster-relief funding. Thank heavens the natural disaster occurred with federal politicians (and their back-room strategists) on their summer break, the counter-productive potential for cynical exploitation of the disaster thus diminished.

Ultimately, this country's future depends on a healthy, well-managed "national" economy with sustainable social policies and the guarantee of equal opportunity for all (if not guaranteed equality of outcome!).

And for all who ponder what they might do "as Prime Minister," a reminder from Plato: "The truth is that if you want a well-governed state to be possible, you must find for your rulers some way of life they like better than government."

From Sea to Sea to Sea:
Take Action with a Mobile
House of Commons

RICHARD ROHMER

RICHARD ROHMER

One of Canada's most highly decorated citizens, Major-General Richard Rohmer is a barrister and best-selling author of 23 fiction and non-fiction books, including *Separation* and *Death by Deficit*. A former Royal Canadian Air Force fighter-reconnaissance pilot and air force general, Richard Rohmer is Chancellor Emeritus of the University of Windsor and military editor emeritus of *The Toronto Sun*. He resides in Collingwood, Ontario, where he is Chair of the Police Services Board. He is a partner in the Toronto law firm of Rohmer and Fenn. He is a Commander of the Order of Military Merit, an officer of the Order of Canada, and a holder of the Distinguished Flying Cross.

As Prime Minister of Canada, I would take new, imaginative, dramatically bold actions to improve the nation's living standards and unite the country.

My first action as First Minister of the national government would be to implement a unity concept that I put forward 20 years ago but my party ignored because it was put forward by a lowly back-bencher—as indeed I then was.

Now, as leader of a majority government, I would be in a position to "persuade" my Cabinet and Caucus to make the great leap forward in the interests of national unity.

The concern for national unity is not single-mindedly focused on the never-ending problems between Quebec and the rest of Canada. Certainly, that relationship is of major importance. But there are also the tangible attitudinal pressures that have been building in British Columbia, where the massive Rocky Mountains and a perceived disregard for British Columbia by Ottawa and its bureaucrats have constructed barriers to unity that compel the independent-minded people of that proud Pacific province to look more and more favourably toward a union with the United States of America.

My "action for unity" concept is totally feasible, based as it is on the use of television, computers, the Internet, and all of the communications technology that the last four years of the 20th century arc bestowing upon our civilization. Combine those instant-communication devices with the modern air-transport facilities that are in place (and ever improving) and you have the foundation elements of my unity concept.

I propose that the House of Commons be made mobile: the Mobile House of Commons. The Mobile House of Commons would be unlocked from Ottawa, which would, of course, remain as the base and bastion of the federal legislature.

The Mobile House would be just that—mobile. It would sit and conduct the nation's parliamentary business in a different major regional city for six weeks in the spring and for six weeks in the fall—or perhaps for eight weeks. That is a detail I would work out with the Leader of the Opposition and the other parties in the House.

The first place of sitting of the Mobile House of Commons could be in British Columbia at a location—probably a conference centre or arena—in Vancouver. Similarly, the second sitting could be in a city in Quebec, such as Montreal. The selected arena or conference centre would be temporarily restructured by transportable seats and furniture modelled on the Ottawa House so that the venue would closely resemble the capital scene.

The Speaker, the clerks, and the entire House staff would be in place at the site of the Mobile House. All members of the House and designated staff could be lifted from Ottawa to the site of the Mobile House in one Boeing 747 or in a series of aircraft.

There is no reason why the House of Commons and the government could not function in the short term just as well in Quebec, Vancouver, Whitehorse, Yellowknife, Calgary, Regina, Winnipeg, Toronto, Halifax, St. John's, or Charlottetown as it does in Ottawa.

What the Mobile House would do for national unity is enormous.

It would force members of Parliament who had little or no exposure or knowledge of regions of Canada other than that of their residence to live in and be involved in regions whose advantages or disadvantages they had never before experienced. As a result of their participation in the Mobile House, members would probably have a totally different understanding of the people, problems, and environment of regions of Canada of which they were not a part or to which they had not been exposed. The citizenry and media of the location of the Mobile House would have first-hand (and likely first-time) experience with the operation of Parliament, even though the Senate would not be part of the scenario. The local citizenry and media would have ready access to members of Parliament and to the committees of Parliament.

Above all, the implementation of my Mobile House of Commons would have the effect of removing the anti-Ottawa syndrome that is pervasive throughout Canada, a nation with various regions that feel remote from, misunderstood, and not cared about by the politicians and bureaucrats who populate Fortress Ottawa and cannot see its gates.

As to communications and the running of the government during a Mobile House session, each minister would be readily available to his or her deputy minister and assistant deputies by means of video-telephone, telephone, fax, and Internet. Airlines serve all of the potential Mobile House locations so there would be ready, quick transportation for Cabinet members, back-benchers, and appropriate staff between Ottawa and the place where the Mobile House is sitting.

Let's imagine that my Cabinet and Caucus have already approved of the operation of the Mobile House on a test basis and the Leader of the Opposition and other party heads have agreed. Accordingly, the first session of the Mobile House, six weeks in all, will be held in Vancouver commencing during the first week in April 1997. The second session of the Mobile House will be held in the fall of 1997 in Montreal.

The challenge of improving the nation's living standards is indeed formidable, because there are so many external or international factors over which the government of Canada has little influence and no control.

My primary focus will be to enhance the opportunities for Canadian companies to find markets for their goods and services in all international areas.

This is not a new objective. It has been both mouthed and pursued by Liberal and Conservative governments continually over the past 40 years. The so-called North American Free Trade Agreement must be revisited with the Americans to make free trade with the United States a reality instead of a Yankee protectionist fiction.

Canadians will improve their living standards only if they increase the sale of goods and services to the United States, Europe, Japan, and the burgeoning nations of Asia and South America. My government will enlarge tax incentives and bonus credits for Canadian companies chasing new business outside the borders of our country. Increased sales mean more jobs, fewer citizens on unemployment insurance and welfare, and an opportunity for everyone to improve his or her standard of living.

It follows that the nation's standard of living and economic health will be improved if the federal government can stop spending more than it takes in. The consequences of continuing to run massive deficits and piling hundreds of millions onto our debt load are fully set out in my "non-fiction novel" *Death by Deficit*, published in 1995. My government will eliminate the annual deficit by 2001 and will then embark on a program to reduce the national debt rapidly and pay it down completely.

My proposals for uniting the country and improving living standards will require enormous efforts on the part of my colleagues and myself. We will do our utmost to succeed to the benefit of all Canadians.

Believe It, Canada

WANDA M. DOROSZ

WANDA M. DOROSZ

Wanda Dorosz is the co-founder, President, and Chief Executive Officer of Quorum Growth Inc., which provides expansion capital and strategic management expertise to growth companies. An author and lecturer on corporate finance, she is a director of numerous Canadian corporations in the public, private, and not-for-profit sectors. She is also a director of Quorum's new Asian subsidiary based in Singapore. Ms. Dorosz is a member of the Advisory Board of Andersen Consulting Inc., the University of Toronto Innovations Foundation, and the University of Toronto Governing Council and Investors Group. She was appointed by the Prime Minister of Canada to the National Advisory Board on Science and Technology, where she served as a member for three years. She holds a law degree from the University of British Columbia.

"If you don't know where you're going,
you can get there anywhere you like."
– *Alice in Wonderland* by Lewis Carrol

Long before nation states ever emerged, great civilizations built their success upon strategy. Theoretically, nation states should accomplish greatness even more easily with the advantages of more definition. However, strategy as the ancients knew it has been relegated to the micro world of the individual, or of private business. Nor does the strategy of the modern military have much to say to the citizens of a Canada today. Therefore, my first act as Prime Minister would be to plan a strategy for a nation, a strategy worthy of the Canada we want. By means of that plan, the dual goals of an improved standard of living and unity would seem less at odds. "Growth, not redistribution" would be the mission of the nation. It would be the chosen theme for Canada as it bridges the two millennia.

Strategy

Strategy is little understood in modern times, particularly in a world such as North America. Here individuals and their rights reign supreme. A collective that unifies people smacks suspiciously of oversimplification, or of brainwashing, or of cheating somebody out of something. Yet never before has there been such a thirst for leadership. Paradoxically, political leadership has never been regarded so poorly. Actually, the sense of paradox is removed when leadership moves up a level to strategy and away from tactical governing. Examples of tactical leadership abound—regional economic redistribution of resources, interest-rate setting, political patronage, duels in the press, and so on.

Yet nation states of this century that think and act strategically know mighty success in short order—Japan, Korea, Singapore, post-

World War II Germany. What they all have in common is a deliberate, nationwide bonding of common goals, more than mere reaction to a crisis such as war or famine or recession.

Why haven't Canadian leaders thought strategically before today? Parts of that answer must lie in the country's youth, its disparate founding peoples, its ability to coast economically on a wealth of natural resources, and the huge, friendly market to the south of us. Yet there has emerged a growing sense of malaise that has manifested itself in a sense of a middle-class tax squeeze, a "Quebec versus the rest of Canada" polarization, a sense of people settling for less. Consequently, we take pride less in what we've done as a nation than in how decent we are as individuals. Pierre Trudeau touched the nation with his "Just Society" mythology. Yet fast forward 30 years: Canadians have a sense that their generosity either has been taken advantage of or has been at too high an economic cost, or both. We fell further behind, not ahead.

Therefore, I believe it is time for all Canadians to choose a future for the nation, not for themselves as individuals. That is what strategy is. Hence, the title of this essay—"Believe It, Canada." No longer can we continue to expect a high standard of living within a united Canada by keeping all of our options open and hoping against hope that merely wishing success will beget success.

Canada must, for the first time in its history, choose and select. Sectorally, we cannot be neutral. Singapore, a mere swampland island that was "kicked out" of Malaysia only 20 years ago, has miraculously transformed itself. It chose to excel in shipping, tourism, telecommunications, and finance. All of its efforts were directed at those goals. It was enormously successful in all.

Canada hasn't dared to make such "political" choices. Therefore, as Prime Minister, I understand I would plan for only one term in office, because the job of tough political choices cannot bridge two terms without "buy-in." Leadership cannot be more than one term ahead of the people. Therefore, I would be prepared to choose sectors that Canada can, or already does, excel in—declare them priorities, put in place infrastructure, and then execute those sectoral strategies throughout all aspects of Canadian life, education, taxation, social benefits, transportation, whatever.

What sectoral strengths does Canada have? Grant us financial systems as one. (Canadian financial institutions can clear cheques through six time zones in the same day.) Another obvious one is telecommunications. An easy third choice is the service industry in the form of engineering. Number four is the fact that Canada is the only nation with borders on three oceans that has never been prioritized as an opportunity. The science of foodstuff is another example of low-hanging fruit.

By contradistinction, manufacturing is not such a good match for a large nation of small population. Similarly, the entertainment industry has little except the tactical advantage of a cheaper Canadian dollar. It is no accident that mighty entertainment industries abound in the populous United States or in Bombay, India. Tourism has potential, but Canada is too seasonal to make the return on the infrastructure needed for sustainable tourism to be as lucrative as that of other nations. Similarly, we lack the historical charm of a Europe to make our cities a tourism differentiation.

The point is not necessarily to be absolutely right about what sectors are the right combination of playing to Canada's strength and being inherently progressive. Rather, it is the very act of selection and the focus that in turn beget a realization of the scarcity of resources, the need to specialize, the need to make alliances, and the need to measure success. Those mental states alone will foster iterative behaviour that allows intelligent moment-to-moment adjustment.

As Prime Minister, I would certainly understand that sectoral choices would need to consider regional strengths. But those choices must not be only historically based. Clear sheet thinking must abound.

Once chosen, the strategy of a better life within a unified nation would then need to extend to the tactics of working a strategy and then to execute the tactics. Canada needn't lose its core values to be tactically successful in executing its chosen strategy. In fact, our decency will make some tactics easier (such as key alliances with other nations). This is how constitutional sores could begin to heal. Constitutional talks must again commence, but with a view to outcomes for all parties five years from today. Clear sheet thinking says that the chosen foundations are redefined. For example, does a common income-tax base still make sense? Should there continue to be regional top-ups between the have and have-not provinces if there is no accountability by the latter to a commonly selected strategy? Provinces can be empowered differently without breaking up the nation if the strategy that powers play to are the same. It's no wonder bitterness has emerged. There's been a sense of "contributing" without a sense of outcome.

Tactics

Once Canada's strategy had chosen simple goals (such as prosperity for all, peace for all, differences for many), then my next act as Prime Minister would be to examine each aspect of the political system in light of its usefulness in attaining the articulated strategy. For example, Canada spends $6 billion annually on research and development not funded by the private sector without any connection to chosen goals. We chose a little of everything but with not enough for anything to really excel globally. Educational paradigms and systems need drastic re-engineering. Should so much of that cost be borne by a land-tax base? Can we afford not to have nationwide standards? Shouldn't some areas be encouraged more than other sectors? Shouldn't the notion of life-long learning be heralded and not cursed? These have an impact on the tax system, labour law, and interprovincial cooperation, let alone an impact on the pillars of education themselves. Once again, the unifying agent of change is an articulated, chosen strategy that is measured after a five-year term. Once measured by a nationwide referendum that is more than marking an "X" for a chosen partisan candidate, the strategy itself, and all the tactical thinking, can be aborted, amended, or continued. But the "nation," Canada, will be united in its desires.

Students of history and of behavourial science can attest to dozen of examples of the success attainable by focus and belief. It's obviously better in the context of strong, individual leaders such as Mahatma Gandhi or Ben Gurion or Franklin Roosevelt. However, I believe that the impact of a single individual as leader is a bit overplayed. Nations that have sustainable prosperity and peace and certainly civilizations of greatness (Rome, China, the British Empire) all had environments that nurtured many generations of leaders. In fact, the progress of Japan this century cannot point to an individual leader who overwhelmingly made a difference. Instead, it was a group of people who came together with an attitude of wanting a better future through common effort.

This leads me to my last act as Prime Minister. Once strategy is set, choices made, infrastructure rethought, referendums established to measure progress, there is still the need to repair the integrity and respect for political office. In non-democratic nations, many successful models abound to prepare leaders for leadership in a formal way. In ancient times, Socrates taught young Greek senators, the Romans trained their Caesars (for example, Marcus Aurelius). In more modern times, aristocracies certainly trained their young to prepare mentally, physically, and spiritually for high office. Some military nation states still prepare their leaders. Something has been lost in modern times, particularly in North America with its notions of universal education and freedom to accomplish anything. Anyone who "wins" electoral office is presumed to have leadership skills, leadership ethics, and, God knows, leadership vision. We must overcome the accusation of elitism and put in place a formal mechanism that will prepare the best and the brightest for office regardless of their walk of life. Once prepared, however, they must be rewarded with privacy that does not remove accountability. They must also be rewarded monetarily for the extra burdens of office.

In conclusion, as Prime Minister I would concentrate on:
- A strategy of choice for all Canadians;
- A strategy that is measured in detail by all every five years by nationwide referendum;
- Clear sheet thinking for all infrastructure of government, especially with a view to playing to our differences as strengths, not weaknesses; and
- Preparing Canadian leaders for the mighty responsibility of leading their people.

Believe it, Canada.

Our Cities, Our Future

PHILIP O'BRIEN

PHILIP O'BRIEN

Philip O'Brien is Chairman and Chief Executive Officer of Devencore Ltd., one of Canada's leading real estate service organizations in the commercial, institutional, and industrial sectors. He is past chairman of the Canadian Chamber of Commerce and a member of the board of trustees of the Canadian Centre for Architecture. He is a member of the executive committee of Le Cercle des chefs meilleurs du Québec and the Business Council on National Issues, Co-Chairman of the Canadian Business Networks Coalition, and a past chairman of the federal Working Committee on Economic Growth Issues. He is also involved in a number of youth and community projects. Mr. O'Brien was the key organizer behind the historic Unity Rally in Montreal on October 27, 1995, prior to the Quebec Referendum.

Our country will change with or without the politicians. The global revolution in communications and technology points to a necessary evolution of Canada's economic organization and suggests a politically neutral opportunity for national unity.

In part, this article is an exploration of the impact that worldwide change, ushered in by new technologies, is having on multinational business. In part, it is an argument for rethinking the central purpose of political leadership, based on my personal experience as a Montreal businessman with a long-standing commitment to the well-being of that city.

It builds on three streams of thought.

The first is the watershed experience of helping organize the Unity Rally held in Montreal before Quebec's October referendum. Concerned citizens demonstrated that they could, and would, act in the absence of professional political leadership.

The second is that technology and communications are redefining personal goals for ordinary people everywhere. Television is showcasing the most advanced economies to the least developed, catalyzing change on a scale that is inevitably global.

Third, for countries seeking to exploit global opportunities, the tools will be city-based, because the major generators of economic activity are nearly always in and around urban centres. In Canada, national or regional governments and political institutions should work to help cities thrive as specialized centres of excellence that export to world markets.

Canada's paths to unity and prosperity are one and the same. Global opportunities and our specific regional resources are the keys to success. We are bound by a global reality that condemns us to succeed or decline.

Five Facts Common to All Canadians

For decades, Canada has been a country of few life-threatening social or political problems. We have been squabblers.

Events did not force most of us to focus on much more than earning a living, educating our children, and getting ahead. We worked hard, but believed we could achieve success on familiar terms and within a well-known social contract.

Our country has sheltered us and allowed us the luxury of complacency. Against the backdrop of tragedies unfolding elsewhere in the world, our difficulties and disputes appeared totally insignificant to bemused outside observers.

But now it appears that global forces are raising the stakes. Chief among them is the powerful impact of technology and communications on our organizations, our cities, and our country as a whole.

All of us will share by necessity in this new adventure thrust upon us. On the one hand it threatens us, some more than others. On the other, it offers tremendous opportunities to rethink our priorities and restructure our central concept of nationhood.

Will we continue to be a country defined by tribal differences, or will we discover that among the many threads of our multicultural society there are uniquely valuable skill-sets with very substantial economic potential on rapidly growing world markets?

If we were willing, furthermore, where would we begin? Well-identified global trends may point to the germ of an answer.

1. The Revolution in Global Marketing

The Cold War is over. There are 1.2 billion people in "First World economies" but four billion more in new, emerging economies whose present resources cannot hope to fill immediate demand for goods, services, or the many layers of service infrastructure that cities in advanced economies take for granted.

Canada's best and brightest corporations are already exporting brand-name products and technologies. They can also export know-how of the kind that will be vital to the health and continued growth of less prosperous populations, from sanitation, transportation, and environmental protection to urban planning and safe regional development.

The result is that Canada's leading companies will inevitably look to the world for the lion's share of their long-term growth. Less attention will be focused on Canadian opportunities alone.

2. The Revolution in Government

Decades of accumulating debt and over-governance, now combined with shrinking populations, are forcing a severe rationalization of government services.

On a parallel track, the corporate world has been forced to trim down as new technologies render entire categories of workers redundant.

Many of us who have traditionally relied on organizations for our livelihood, and on government support when all else failed, realize we may have neither. Large sectors of the population feel abandoned and are seeking something—anything—for which they can work and with whose interests they can identify.

The traditional social contract is being eroded by global forces; a new form of contract will surely take root. We must manage the opportunity.

3. The Information Revolution and Global Identity

Information technology is immediately and globally distributed. CNN, Windows '95, Hollywood, and Silicone Valley are all information-based and by their nature exert tremendous pressures for change. They are at heart industries of ideas and know-how.

Thus, an Indian or a Mexican family can now afford a tricycle for a child, but their ambition is to own a personal computer. With that one tool, parents and children win access to a world of opportunity previously locked away.

People like these are obvious clients for displaced high-tech workers in North America. Canada's displaced knowledge workers will become of necessity "information nomads," self-reliant, technically skilled, and actively seeking to be engaged in the new world economy.

4. The Social Revolution and Tribal Identity

As traditional socioeconomic contracts wear away, unskilled workers see little hope for a gainful future. Great numbers are searching for a force, a cult, a religion, or a provider that will restore their hope and lead them in a direction where they will find their own place in the new economic order.

5. The Evolution of the Regional Economy

As these forces move forward, we have the setting for either conflict or resolution. The instinct of the alienated, non-skilled population is to withdraw inward. By necessity, displaced knowledge workers must look outward.

Each group is an important human resource. Each can be found in the same regions and in the same cities. As a nation, we must devise economic, social, and political structures that accommodate everyone or face tremendous urban strife and the potential dismemberment of our country.

The city-centred regional economy will be a child of the meltdown. It is in cities that the array of talent and expertise is concentrated and the necessary infrastructure exists to retrain and harness untapped human potential.

It is in cities, I would argue, where national governments must join with the private sector to build systems to showcase and market Canadian talent and resources.

Finding Opportunities Instead of Problems

Evolution of the Regional Economy

Global opportunities for business are no longer for multinationals alone. They exist, they are available today, and they are effectively open to any who will look for them and spend the time to address them.

What most of us need is the appropriate channel to market our products. With enormous resources on tap, multinational corporations are well placed to scout the world for new business. But we are very much a nation of small business. Should smaller entrepreneurs be looking outside their own territories for new customers?

I believe the answer is an emphatic "Yes!" Cities, the hubs of regional economies, offer the natural launching pad for several reasons.

- The meltdown of traditional government funding has sharply reduced federal or provincial payments to urban centres, but the expense of maintaining complex infrastructures remains. New markets mean new revenues.
- We already have clusters of excellence in various regions of the country, concentrated and showcased in major cities. All cities have unique assets of geography and resources. All have developed a particular blend of industry, distribution, and know-how as a result. All have populations of varied cultures that have found shared commitments on common ground.
- Cities are at the same time the seeds of a new form of national identity: closer to the people, faster to adjust. It is to their city, to their home, that most people give first allegiance. It is in the city region that we live and work.
- Within the municipalities of large cities, there is traditional competition for new business. With effective global marketing strategies, much nonproductive competition could be avoided.
- By contrast, most cities can afford to be tolerant of the strengths of other centres. With effective coordination, each can become an effective niche player, selling its own specialities to its neighbours while simultaneously marketing them abroad.

Here is a vital opportunity for governments to provide meaningful support. We need to further develop visible, user-friendly channels for entrepreneurs in regional economies, for obtaining information, promoting new supplier/customer networks, and supplying useful counselling on legal or banking standards in foreign markets. Most of all, we need top-down commitment to the idea that our cities hold the key to economic and social renaissance of our own country.

The Global City

We see the global city as an urban region, self-sufficient and with a long-range strategy to market itself internationally.

In a new world economy that provides enormous opportunities but demands a truly entrepreneurial willingness to adapt, leadership in global cities must find ways to harmonize the aspirations and needs of both traditional and knowledge workers. The goal should be to create and export both know-how and product worldwide.

We need a strong, working partnership between private and public sectors, driven by a common vision that our cities are multifaceted products in need of a marketing plan.

The City Partnership

In emerging economies around the world, technology has empowered local business. In a few, short years, urban centres that languished for most of the century have come alive with new investment. Industry has flourished and spun off tremendous local prosperity.

In New Delhi, for example, planners are expecting more than 1,000,000 new inhabitants before the end of the century and some 2,000 extra vehicles arrive on the streets every month. But the city was congested to begin with and most of its infrastructure seriously outdated.

Public transportation, telephone service, inadequate utilities, and pollution have become serious problems. Canada, on the other hand, consistently ranks near the top worldwide in quality of urban life. We have expertise to sell and potential customers awaiting.

Rapidly growing cities face similar crises in other countries. Inadequate construction regulations may allow buildings to collapse. Social and medical services may be non-existent. In fact, much of the social and urban planning know-how we have developed over decades simply has not been affordable for developing cities—and it doesn't exist.

From port management to energy distribution, public health to education, Canadian cities have unique expertise to offer the emerging regional economies of the world.

City partnership is the concept that we can bring the energy of our own skilled people together to build linkages, create growth opportunities, and celebrate our differences by combining them for export.

We have the opportunity in Canada to use the strengths of our own urban centres to rebuild our regional economies, improve the lives of others, and enrich our relationships with each other.

A Montreal Experience

I live in a city that has been held hostage for the last 25 years. Politically, it has been captive to the nationalist ambitions of Quebec City. Economically, it has been at the mercy of Ottawa's conviction that regional interests must be subordinate to national policy.

In essence, Ottawa and Quebec have been so busy fighting ancient battles that neither has effectively tuned in to a global agenda, nor focused on global opportunities.

During the last Quebec referendum campaign, it became apparent to many of us that the political establishments in Ottawa and Quebec City were obsessed with a dispute that held no benefits for Montreal. A city that was one of the wealthiest on the continent was being sacrificed to political rhetoric.

As one of a group of people working for the No Committee, I was asked by politicians to organize a rally at our convention centre for "2,000 people in suits." The organizers wanted a photo opportunity.

We set about gathering not just people in suits, but also people with intelligence and conviction. A number of committed Montrealers joined in the effort.

To our dismay, we found out an hour before the event was to start that someone had cut down the size of the hall to half capacity, fearing that fewer people than expected would show up. In fact, about 4,500 people appeared and most of them couldn't get into the room. An editorial writer from the Montreal *Gazette* asked me what was going on. Apparently the same political organizers had not informed them of the event, again fearing a public relations dud.

Under Quebec's referendum legislation, we had been operating under strict financial constraints and had spent the $3,000 we had been allowed. But the turn-out demonstrated what all of us already believed: that there were a great many Montrealers determined to express support for their city and for Canada once given the opportunity.

So we met again, to organize a second event that would cost nothing: a public rally held outside at no expense to anyone. We decided to ask any and all who shared our views to join in, whether from Montreal, Quebec City, La Beauce, or anywhere else in the province.

Thousands of people got involved, from all sides of the community, and it rapidly became obvious that, quite by accident, we had discovered how to move people in a way the government establishment no longer understood—the role cities can play in nation-building.

We were providing a way for the empowerment of individual citizens, a reason for them to work to achieve a goal that was clearly perceived and highly valued.

The Unity Rally was a watershed event. It was a powerful expression of solidarity among Canadians and the perhaps first page in a new chapter of Montreal history. Montrealers had taken responsibility for their city while the political hierarchy pursued its obsession with established political context. In so doing, Montrealers had mobilized nationwide support and possibly shown themselves how their city could take its first steps to becoming, once again, a "global city."

A Proposal

Perhaps the time has come to rethink our political structures. If the only way Montreal can get results is for its own population to bypass the political "powers that be," that city is not getting the representation it deserves. Would other cities fare any better under similar circumstances?

If Canada is to prosper in the new global economy, if Canada is to remain united, we will need a political body mandated to specifically represent urban interests.

Why not rethink the role of the Senate with this objective in mind? Why not look for strategic solutions—for instruments of government that benefit us all by welcoming and merchandizing our regional differences?

We don't need to waste more time arguing on how to divide the pie. We simply need to start cooking!

Note: Many of the ideas expressed here are not only the author's. They have been gathered from media reports, published articles, and a great many discussions with friends and business associates. Many thanks to everyone involved.

Index

marketing, global, 210
McGill University, 147
medical care Health care
Meech Lake, 12, 161, 184
Memorial University, 93
military service, 69
monarchy, eliminating, 98
multiculturalism, 48, 67
  terminating programs, 69

National Energy program, 67
National Youth Corps, 22–23
national defence, 22
national service, 69
national unity, 11–13, 19–22, 69, 80–86
  barriers to, 191
  developing, 67–68
  division of powers and, 21–22
  and Saguenay flood, 185
  Tripartite Confederate Assembly and, 19–21
natural resources, 163
No Committee, 215
North American Free Trade Agreement, 193

Osgoode Hall Law School, 65
Oxford University, 169

Parliament, changing structure, 20–21, 35–40
parliamentary system, changes to, 80–86
partisan politics, problems with, 34
pension plans, private, 9
poverty, among children, 177
power
  abuse of, 56
  devolution of, 151, 154
  diluting, 59
  preventing corruption of, 56, 59
powers, federal and provincial, 132, 151. See
  also Provincial powers
pride, in being Canadian, 48, 49, 69
Prime Minister
  as head of state, 98
  limiting terms of, 39
  qualities of, 50
  role of, 105
privatization
  of Canada Pension Plan, 8, 9
  of Canadian Broadcasting Corporation, 8
  demands for, 55
  of Department of National Defence, 11
  of federal government operations, 5–11,
    12, 13
  of foreign aid, 8
  of health care, 13
  of unemployment insurance, 8
productivity, 115, 118, 132, 173
Progressive Conservative Youth Association, 5
proportional representation, 68, 83, 86, 97
  advantages of, 83
  costs of, 87
  disadvantages of, 83, 85

provinces
  and accounting, 177
  transfers to, 10
provincial powers
  delegating to federal government, 95
  equality of, 108
  increasing, 22

Quebec
  avoiding referendum in, 49
  as distinct society, 171
  equalization payments to, 11–12
  improving relations with, 45
  nationalists, 19
  protecting culture, 50
  and referendum, 171, 185, 197, 209, 215
  separation of, 11, 12, 107, 161, 185
  separatism, 67, 73–74
  special rights, 49
Queen's University, 127
Queen, eliminating role of, 98
Quorum Growth Inc., 197

railways, importance of, 130
redistribution, 199
referendum
  guidelines for, 107
  nationwide, 202, 203
  and Quebec, 171, 185, 197, 209, 215
  on separation, 12
  for stalemated issues, 84
regional conflict, reducing, 19, 96
regional development, 22
regional economy, 212–213
regional strengths, 201
rent stamps, 46
research and development, 202
resource use, 45, 142
responsibilities, federal and provincial, 149
retirement planning, 9, 110
RRSPs, 71, 110

St. Lawrence Seaway, 129
Saint Mary's University, 43
Securities and Exchange Commission, 153
self-government for Aboriginal peoples, 96,
  97, 108, 143
Senate
  abolishing, 68, 83, 84, 87
  Aboriginal people in, 109
  length of term in, 106
  powers of, 21
  reforming, 20, 97, 105–106
  relations with House of Commons, 21, 106
  "Triple-E," 20
  weakness of, 19–20
seniors' benefits, replacing, 109
separation, 55
  of provinces and territories, 164
  of Quebec, 11–12, 107, 109
separatist movement in Quebec, 13, 50

The Magna For Canada Scholarship Fund

In 1995, Magna International Inc., placed one million dollars in a trust to establish the Magna For Canada Scholarship Fund, an annual awards program for Canadian college and university students. The program is designed to provide a national forum for new and innovative ideas for creating a more prosperous country.

The Scholarship Fund provides cash awards each year to ten regional winners from across the country, one of whom is selected as the national champion at a Gala Awards evening. In addition to the student winners, up to ten recognized Canadians are also asked to submit proposals in the special Invitational category.

The awards program is sponsored by Magna International Inc., Canada's largest supplier of automotive systems and components. For more information on the Magna For Canada Scholarship Fund, including details on how to participate in this year's competition, please call 1-800-976-2462.

The Fair Enterprise Institute

The Magna For Canada Scholarship Fund is endorsed by the Fair Enterprise Institute, a non-profit, non-partisan policy research organization founded to improve Canadian living standards.

The Institute's mandate is to initiate public discussion and provide policy alternatives through forums and programs such as the Magna For Canada Scholarship Fund. The Fair Enterprise Institute will also generate policy proposals on a wide range of socio-economic and political issues that have a direct bearing on the economic well-being of Canadians.

Fair Enterprise is an economic philosophy based on a business charter of rights which has as its core principle the pre-determined distribution of profits between management, employees and shareholders, and which also gives employees the right of equity participation. These rights are designed to motivate the company's key stakeholders for greater productivity and participation in the growth of the business.